Using
literature
with
young
children

Using literature with young children

edited by Leland B. Jacobs

TEACHERS COLLEGE PRESS
TEACHERS COLLEGE, COLUMBIA UNIVERSITY
NEW YORK AND LONDON

CONTENTS

Enjoying literature

with young children

For literature to be enjoyable to the young, it takes an appealing book, an eager child, a comfortable setting, and a sensitive, enthusiastic adult. Without any one of these components, the experience is likely to be less than satisfying. For literature does not just happen in a child's life. It is in his days because an adult who really cares about children and books gets them together under the best possible conditions.

KINDS OF BOOKS FOR YOUNG CHILDREN

There are four general kinds of books for young children: informational books, "mood" literature, fiction, and poetry.

Informational books do just what the title suggests—they inform. The information may be about the natural world, the scientific world, the man-made world. Whatever its content, informational books for young children should be factually accurate, free from careless over-generalization or facts too tightly packed in, and written in a style that is precise but not pedantic.

"Mood" literature deals more with concepts, or with feelings about something in the common experience of young children. It relies on a rhythmic, descriptive prose patterning to create sights and sensations that suggest rather than state observations about life or the world with which it is dealing. Rather than relate facts and information, a "mood" book sensitizes the young to what is already somewhat known in ways that lift the knowing above the ordinary or mundane.

This chapter is by LELAND B. JACOBS, of Teachers College, Columbia University.

1

Fiction, whether realistic or fanciful, provides a true story line. A character, in a recognizable or imaginable setting, moves through a series of actions in which there is such complication that a solution has to come about. Fiction for young children may be in either a "believe" or a "make-believe" mode. It may be old stories that have come down, through time, from the oral storytelling tradition, or stories of very recent creation. But fiction for young children, no matter what else it may be, should be good fiction, written with integrity, validity, simplicity, and beauty.

Poetry gives young children what Coleridge calls "the best words in their best order," or what Robert Frost calls "a performance in words." From Mother Goose rhymes to selected works of such established poets as Walter de la Mare and John Ciardi, poetry deserves a distinctive place in the balanced literature program for young children. Joy in sound, in imagery, in time and tempo, in mood is poetry's to give.

The young child deserves many opportunities to get acquainted with all four general kinds of books. Thus he learns to know the many faces of enjoyment through literature—the enjoyment of being knowledgeable both in fact and feeling, the enjoyment of language gloriously used, the enjoyment of moments of heightened sensitivity to life and living.

PICTURES ARE IMPORTANT

In books for young children, the pictures are important. In fact, the illustrations are integral in the total content of the book. In informational books, the pictures may fill in details of information that the prose text does not give explicitly, or they may reinforce information already given by presenting it in a different form. In "mood" literature, the concepts or feelings are given added dimensions in line and space, and in shading and color. In poetry, the essence of the poetic moments is punctuated or epitomized in pictures. In fiction, the illustrations complement the text by telling the story also in their own way.

As one studies the art in these books he may well ask, critically:

- Will these pictures attract and hold the attention of the intended audience?

- Will they entertain and re-entertain?

- Are they truly essential to the content?

- Do they catch the mood and feeling of the writing?

- Are the pictures rightly placed to augment the text?

- Are the pictures done in an appropriate medium?

In the most enjoyable literature for young children, a harmony of print and pictures is achieved. One can read the pictures right along with the print. Or one can read the print through the pictures. The artist is a necessary partner in the creation of the book.

CHILDREN AND BOOKS TOGETHER

Bringing children and books together is the pleasant task of the teacher. This means that the teacher not only knows books but also the children for whom the books are intended. What are these particular children like? What do their free-choice activities and talk indicate might appeal to them? What books might be attractive to them as a confirmation of their experience? Which might appeal as an extension of their experience?

The timing of the presentation of a book to young children is clear in the case of seasonal or holiday content. For other kinds of content, timing depends on the astuteness of the teacher's observation as to the appropriateness of the book in content appeal, in vocabulary, and in length. If the teacher has made a mistake in judgment, however, it is easily rectified. For the children will let one know that they do not care for the selection, and the book can be put aside, to be tried again, perhaps, some other time.

The setting and physical arrangements for sharing a book with children are important. Before a book is shared, time is well spent to see that children are comfortable, that there will be eye contact between child and teacher, that children who disturb each other are not together, and so forth. Thus a minimum of disruptions is assured. The book is given a chance to be its best.

Too, the setting for individual perusal of books is important. The young child needs to have books shared with him, where he is an active listener and viewer. But he also needs time to be contemplative with books—to turn their pages at his own rate, to study the pictures at close range, to recall the content for his own pleasure. Actual space for group enjoyment or individual pleasure with books is essential. "Psychological space," room to move about in one's mind with the writer, must also be assured by the mood and spirit created, if the young child is to receive books unto himself.

The young child's enjoyment of literature is stimulated by the enthusiasm of the adults who introduce books to him. For full enjoyment of books, they must be shared with someone who also enjoys the experience. Hearing prose and poetry read aloud, looking at pictures together, discussing what a book prompts children to want to talk about, rereading favorites—these are activities in which an adult makes possible the pleasure that books can bring into the child's experience.

But all this means that the adult must be genuinely enthusiastic. Hence, the teacher will avoid trying to share what he himself does not really enjoy and appreciate. Nor will he try to present to children either prose or poetry with which he is not fully familiar. And surely he will eschew following a prescribed list of books and selections for a particular age or grade level, or any other practice that emanates from a sense of "duty" rather than from ardor and respect. One does not fool children by pretense at enthusiasm. They see through any such artificiality most perceptively. On the other hand, what exhilaration can become theirs when, with observable joy in the doing, the teacher shares that literature which is impelling and aesthetically satisfying to him as well as appropriate for the children.

LITERATURE AND KNOWING

Young children want to know, and prose and poetry can help children know in many ways. It can take them deeper into information concerning the natural and man-made world, about which they already have some knowledge. It can help them refine concepts and insights. It can take them into experiences which they have never, at first hand, had. It can take them into imaginary places and circumstances that give them a distinctive, extraordinary vision of what is beyond the reach of the familiar. It can help them look at happenings and things commonplace to them with fresh and enlarged comprehension and appreciation. It can help them know more about life and nature, man and men, and "I" and "Thou."

Informational books will make their contribution to young children's knowing by quite logical means. Here the child is guided directly by the writer to facts, generalizations, observations; so he will be better informed. In these books, the writer uses straight discourse to help his readers to know more. The child becomes more analytically knowledgeable.

In fiction and poetry the writer relies on imagination and aesthetic impact in reaching the young child. He orders some components of existence in such ways that the child feels what the writer is communicating. He responds to the writer's creation of mood, comparison, character, incident, place, or time. The child does not come to know logically from experience with fiction or poetry. Rather, he feels what it is like to be in the presence of what has been imaginatively created by the writer. The child feels the impact of something in life—laughter, tears, pity, despair, solutions of problems, fulfillment of desires, love—as the author has delineated it. He is "caught up" in the mood, the situations, the dilemmas, the perceptions, the happenings as if they were immediate, forceful, real.

4

The child, for the moment, is not himself. He becomes what the writer wants him to be. He intuitively knows, through his identification and response, what the writer would help him to know: what it is like to be Peter Rabbit, to go "hoppity," to observe a turtle that snaps at a flea, to be The Little House, or Little Toot the tug boat. While fiction or poetry is respectful of facts, neither is a factual presentation. Both are symbolic representations of life. And the child knows about affection, acceptance, and approval; knows about approaches and confrontations in human destiny; knows about how facts feel in action and how information and misinformation influence man's behavior, his coping with his world.

As young children enjoy the informational and the fictional or poetic, they are broadening and deepening their bases for knowing: for understanding and inquiring, for pondering and pretending, for illuminating their experiences through increased factual knowledge and increased sensibilities to that which is human and humane. Thus they will learn early to look to literature for truth and wisdom as well as for aesthetic impact, with respectful curiosity for the many faces of the human relationship and the foibles and wonders of man as he makes his way to meanings in existence.

If there is skepticism that books for young children can achieve such worthy ends, then one hastily adds that not all books will contribute so much, but rather that well-selected, first-rate books can, and enjoyably so.

With good books in plentiful supply, and reasonable conditions for a healthful physical, psychological, and intellectual climate, and eager, zestful children, what more is needed if young children are to enjoy literature? The leaven: a perceptive teacher who gives "the treasure for the taking."

Providing good literature

for young children

The care that a teacher of young children puts into providing good literature for the group will "pay off" in the children's heightened interest in reading and in developing embryonic literary taste. One of the first steps is to provide a library center in the classroom.

THE ROOM LIBRARY

Whether or not a school or public library is accessible, it is important to make such provisions within nursery school, kindergarten, and primary classrooms.

The location of the library in a somewhat separated and relatively quiet spot in the room will contribute to an atmosphere of seclusion. Screens, bookcases, movable bulletin boards or cupboards may be so arranged as to provide the desired feeling of separation from other activities. This does not mean, however, that silence must reign in a library. A children's room in a public library once bore the sign, BE STILL AND LET THY VOICE BE LOW. Resistence to this admonition became evident when a child surreptitiously inserted an l in the space between the words BE and LOW! The sharing of enthusiasm among children over their books is one of the chief means of arousing interest in books. But children cannot share enthusiasm in silence. Teachers have observed that numerous "reluctant readers" are won over by other children while resisting all efforts of their teachers to involve them.

The room library must be well lighted and should be a cheerful and inviting place. It should be possible here to achieve either a private, in-

---

This chapter is by RUTH E. GREEN, of the University of Minnesota, Duluth.

dividual experience or a social one. Sometimes a teacher may provide special, comfortable furniture for this center. One teacher fastened three old kindergarten chairs together, padded it liberally with foam rubber, covered it with bright chintz and thus achieved an attractive, comfortable, child-sized studio couch. This was a favorite spot for children to "settle down with books." Other teachers (or the children's mothers) have made attractive slip covers for the backs of chairs in the library center. Another teacher likes to keep an ever-changing, attractive centerpiece on the library table. In one room library is a shelf reserved for visiting "storybook dolls" or figurines.

Books should be easily reached and replaced. One or more small tables should be provided because many of the books for young children are large and are difficult to hold on the lap.

A bulletin board may be used to display jackets of new books, children's illustrations of stories and poems, pictures of authors and illustrators, the rare and precious letter from a favorite author or a carefully lettered poem with accompanying picture. A globe and maps are frequently a part of the room library.

SELECTING BOOKS FOR THE ROOM LIBRARY

If literary taste is to develop, if children's varying interests and reading needs are to be met, if reading skills are to be strengthened through supplementary reading, the books in the room library must be carefully selected.

There is nothing enticing, for most young children, about a collection of tattered, dull-colored, haphazardly arranged books. The attractive format of a book is the first invitation to children to pick it up and look through it or read it. The neat, but not stiff, arrangement of books on the shelves also serves to attract children to their use.

The primary concern, of course, is for the content of these books. With the great number of really excellent books available for young children, the books in the room library need not be of mediocre quality.

Teachers of beginning reading have long wished for story books which are simple enough for these young children to read independently and yet have more interesting content and story appeal than the usual primers and first readers can provide. At the present time a great many such attempts are on the market, a number of which are well done. It should be remembered, however, that strict vocabulary control is not necessary for all young readers, and also that adults should continue to read high-level literature to children. This is as necessary as it is for children to see good art and to hear good music beyond their abilities to produce themselves.

The teacher will need to provide a variety of types of literature as well as variety in subject matter and in reading level. A well-balanced room collection might include:

- Some good Mother Goose and ABC books.

- Classics, enjoyed by generations of readers.

- New books with fresh, different approaches.

- Some humorous, even ridiculous, stories—"just for fun."

- Much realism, but also

- Some touches of the fanciful.

- Books of information to which children will turn for the answering of questions and the satisfying of their need *to know*.

- Some well-illustrated anthologies of poetry and single authors' collections. (As a rule, poetry is best enjoyed and appreciated as an oral experience, but many children enjoy poring over the pictures and recalling poems they have heard. To include poetry in the literature available to children helps to build the concept that poetry "belongs" and is an important part of literary experience.)

- Many picture books with slight text, particularly in the nursery school or kindergarten library.

The teacher has available a number of good guides to selecting children's literature. The teacher's own perception and taste can be one of his best resources. This is a subtle ability but can be developed through a good background in appreciation of adult literature and through the study of "Children's Literature." Such a course is offered in most teacher-preparing institutions. An "in-service" teacher, however, may take several additional steps. Numerous good textbooks exist which discuss and evaluate children's books. Carefully prepared bibliographies are available from such organizations as the Association for Childhood Education, The National Council of Teachers of English, The Child Study Association, and the American Library Association. Children's Book Clubs are growing, and a number of them provide quite adequate selections. Reviews of current books appear regularly in such periodicals as *The Horn Book, Elementary English,* and *Childhood Education.*

A teacher should, of course, examine the books themselves rather than rely entirely on annotations or book reviews. Book Exhibits and Book Fairs are becoming more easily available and the quality of the books displayed is improving. Here teachers may look over a wide selection of current publications.

USING AND CARING FOR BOOKS

"But books are to be read to out of!" wailed a young child whose baby-sitter had sent him to his room with a stack of carefully selected library books, with the hope that she—the baby-sitter—might get at her school work. It is not enough to furnish the books and the space. The teacher must also provide:

- Time and encouragement to browse and to read. Such "leisure" reading should be considered a very respectable expenditure of school time.

- Opportunities for children and teacher to share stories and poems. The teacher's reading to children is a valuable part of the language arts program.

- Opportunities for the children to express their reactions to their reading and listening experiences. These may include very informal "reports" (oral and written), illustrations, or conversations. The writing of book reviews from stilted, stereotyped outlines is not desirable.

- Opportunities to teach children to care for the books.

Children will not learn to appreciate and care for books by being allowed to drop them, throw them onto the shelves and tables, slide them across the floor, or handle them with dirty, sticky hands. On the other hand, children will not be attracted to books if their handling of them is too throughly restricted. The locking of attractive new books into an inaccessible bookcase, or a teacher's continual cautioning and hovering, will result in repelling rather than attracting children to books. Books are to be handled and read. School personnel must recognize that books, through much normal handling by many children, *will* become worn and will need to be replaced. Children must be taught to exercise care, of course. The teacher's example in handling the books with care and respect will do much to lead the children to do so, also. In addition, avoiding crowded conditions and excessive competition for the books, providing unobtrusive but effective supervision, and instilling the attitude that browsing and reading are daily *privileges* (not punishments or "time-passers") will all help to develop proper attitudes and the accompanying care in the use of books.

The provision of good literature in the early school years is an extremely important function of the school. The test of a good reading program is not only that the children *can* read, but they *do* read—beyond the minimum required of them. If young children in their pre-reading and early reading years learn to turn to and enjoy good books, they will have taken a giant step toward this objective.

SELECTED READINGS

Arbuthnot, May Hill. *Children and Books.* Revised edition. Chicago: Scott, Foresman and Company, 1957. Chapter 4, "Mother Goose"; Chapter 6, "Verses in the Gay Tradition"; Chapter 7, "Poetry of the Child's World"; Chapter 8, "Singing Words"; Chapter 11, "Old Magic"; Chapter 14, "New Magic"; Chapter 15, "Here and Now"; Chapter 17, "Animal Stories."

Association for Supervision and Curriculum Development. (Prepared by Harold G. Shane.) *Research Helps in Teaching the Language Arts.* Washington, D.C.: National Education Association, 1955. Chapter 7, "The Care and Feeding of Bookworms."

Duff, Annis. *Bequest of Wings.* New York: Viking Press, 1944.

Eakin, Mary K. *Good Books for Children.* Chicago: University of Chicago Press, 1962. (Also available in paperback edition.)

Fenner, Phyllis. *The Proof of the Pudding: What Children Read.* New York: John Day Company, 1957.

Frank, Josette. *Your Child's Reading Today.* Garden City, N. Y.: Doubleday and Company, 1954.

Herrick, Virgil E., and Jacobs, Leland B. *Children and the Language Arts.* Englewood Cliffs, N. J.: Prentice-Hall, Inc., 1955. Chapter 9, "Children's Experiences in Literature."

Huck, Charlotte S., and Young, Doris A. *Children's Literature in the Elementary School.* New York: Holt, Rinehart and Winston, 1961. Part II, "Knowing Children's Literature."

Larrick, Nancy. *A Teacher's Guide to Children's Books.* Columbus, Ohio: Charles E. Merrill, 1960. Chapter 1, "Children and Books in the First Grade"; Chapter 2, "As Children Begin to Read"; Chapter 3, "In Grades Two and Three"; Chapter 7, "Poetry Has a Special Place"; Chapter 16, "Favorite Books for Boys and Girls."

Walsh, Frances. *That Eager Zest.* Philadelphia: J. B. Lippincott Company, 1961.

Reading aloud

to young children

Those who read to children accept both a wonderful opportunity and a fair-sized responsibility. For through reading aloud to young children one can share the joy and wonder of broadening acquaintances in the world of books and whet their appetites for more stories and poems as well as influence—hopefully—their literary tastes that will last a lifetime.

Through reading aloud, the reader re-creates for children not only their own world seen through other eyes but leads them, also, to worlds beyond the eye. Reading aloud is a way to let children enter, vicariously, into a larger world—both real and fanciful—in company with an adult who cares enough to take them on the literary journey.

Since the child's introduction to books is controlled by adult choices, books of quality, varied in style and text, should be his to know. These books will undoubtedly be beyond his present reading ability; however, reading aloud enables him to enjoy and appreciate what he could not manage on his own. Moreover, it probably extends his vocabulary; develops fond memories of stories and poems; gives him a feeling for the beauty of language; and arouses a desire to read on his part. He comes to know man's experiences in many situations, places, and activities. And he has only to give himself to the listening.

How much better it is for the young one to sit back and enjoy listening to *Winnie the Pooh* or "The Elephant's Child" rather than struggle with Milne's sentence structure or Kipling's vocabulary. The warmth of the reader's voice and his ability to highlight and give substance to the

This chapter is by KAY VANDERGRIFT, of the Agnes Russell School, Teachers College, Columbia University.

selection not only facilitate the child's interpretation of the story, but at the same time serve as a model and an incentive for his own reading.

SELECTING STORIES AND POEMS

Selection is not, basically, a matter of paging through available books shortly before the reading time or even of choosing starred titles from standard reading lists. One who truly delights in fine literature for children and is sincerely concerned with the young children with whom he works will continually be alert for prose and poetry which he himself enjoys and which will be, according to his insights, right for his particular group of children. As he comes to know these children, he will be able to anticipate certain concerns and reactions and build a collection of stories to meet these needs. There is a thrill in sharing a story or poem related to a specific incident immediately as it occurs, as well as in appropriately opening up the wonders of a world that is new and potentially appealing.

Any story worthy of the time spent in reading should offer something of significance to the listeners. Perhaps the teacher is merely filling a gap in the day's activities, but one need not fill it with the mediocre. Some selections will undoubtedly be read for informational content; these too must be judged with an eye to their literary quality. Even though a book presents facts, if it does not do so in a clearly superior manner, a teacher is probably better off depending upon his own presentation.

Frequently a story will have certain inherent qualities which are better shared through reading aloud than through storytelling. Many picture-story books should be read rather than told, since the illustrations are an integral part of the story. Other stories call for the exact words or style of the author or for a certain innate rhythm which might be lost in the telling. Most storytellers are able to entrance a young audience with their own telling of the action of *The Three Billy Goats Gruff,* but who would dare to compete with Seuss' own telling of *Horton Hatches the Egg?*

These inherent qualities are especially important in poetry. Imagine "telling" a poem to children. Whether a poem is memorized or interpretatively read, one must present it as it is, for it is not only the verbal statement that is important, but the exact phrasing and a singing quality of rhythm, and perhaps rhyme, as well.

Gradually, as children become familiar with the literature that is their heritage, they will begin to make their own selections for the story hour. Along with those books chosen by the adult, they may ask to return to the familiar settings or the strong rhythms and repetitions of a story or poem enjoyed previously.

PREPARATION FOR READING

The best preparation for anyone who reads to children is not only to know the story well, but to enjoy it thoroughly and to feel strongly about it. Thoughtful silent reading will familiarize him with the sequence of events, the mood and tempo of the story, and the author's distinctive vocabulary. Then reading aloud will enable him to adjust the expression, the timing, and the emphasis to his own voice quality. One just beginning to read to others will find it especially valuable to listen to his own voice on tape before facing a young audience.

As one prepares for reading aloud to young children, he needs to take into account the mood, viewpoint, and spirit he wishes to establish in his reading, as well as how he will pace his presentation. Too, he will want to consider how to prepare the children to anticipate a "believe" or "make believe" situation, and what, if any, follow-up discussion or other activities he plans to use. However, no amount of preparation can make up for a lack of sincerity on the part of the reader. That which is read with feeling will almost always be listened to with respect.

PROVIDING A SUITABLE SETTING

Once the story is chosen and prepared, the reader must select a suitable setting for its presentation. There might be a "story corner" or some area set aside for the reading and telling of stories. This could be an informal and comfortable area—possibly a few pillows arranged on the floor, a fluffy rug, or a rocking chair—where children can relax and enjoy literature. Most youngsters relish a bit of ritual with their story hour, perhaps the lighting of a "story candle" or a certain quiet time each day when they can expect to share a story with the entire group. Although it may be wise to set aside this time free from interruptions, this should not be the only time literature is shared, nor should it become inflexible. Those "occasional" stories selected for the children may find their way into any part of the day, and even the scheduled story hour varies with the particular book, the interests of the children, and the total plans of the day.

USE OF PICTURES IN READING

As mentioned previously, many picture books demand that children be able to follow the illustrations as the text is read to them. It is important that the reader learn to hold these oversized books comfortably, so the pictures are easily seen as he reads. He may point out certain details as they are mentioned in the story if this does not disturb the children's viewing or sidetrack attention from the selection. Since the pictures are an integral part of the story, listeners need to digest these as well as the text. Sufficient time is needed to take them in. Thus, a book which could literally be "read" in a minute or two may require much more time when it is really "read" to young children.

Only pictures that are large, clear, and easily seen should be used with a whole group. It is far better for the listener to conjure up his own images than to strain to see those shown by the reader. Wanda Gág's *Millions of Cats* is a delight to see, but the illustrations are too small and detailed to be absorbed in a group situation. With this particular book, it might be advisable to show the filmstrip as the text is read and save the book itself for reading to one or two children.

SUGGESTIONS FOR THE READING ITSELF

"Reading Aloud" time has come. An unhurried atmosphere is established. Listeners are seated comfortably on low chairs or pillows where their faces can be seen as well as the book. The reader has prepared the group for those new words or concepts necessary for the understanding of the story. He reads. Although just a bit slower than normal speech, the tone is that of a relaxed conversationalist. Dramatic passages are interpreted naturally and different characters speak with slightly different voices, but there is no overacting. During the reading, a parenthetical phrase may be added as the reader notes puzzlement on young faces, but he doesn't stop to explain while telling the story.

Entering into the story, children may begin to laugh or make comments about the action. These are acknowledged by a smile or a nod and the slight pause required in the reading. The child whose attention is beginning to wander can often be drawn back into the group by that smile or by softly mentioning his name. The reader's enjoyment of his story is evident; his listeners share that enjoyment with him.

The story ends; the children go back to the day's activities. But sometime later one may find that reading together isn't something that is finished when the final page has been read. The book is closed, but the world found there remains. Long afterward a phrase or a gesture may take one back to live again in that world and share anew the pleasures of "Once upon a time . . ." or "On a snowy city street . . ."

Telling stories

to young children

Everyone who works with young children is called upon to be a storyteller. "Tell us a story!" has been the perennial plea of generations of
youngsters. And anyone who works with young children can be a storyteller—even a better storyteller than he sometimes thinks he can. But as
he develops his art, he will do well to give thought to what a storyteller
really is; how a good storyteller makes his preparation; how a good storyteller selects his material; and how he does the telling.

WHAT A STORYTELLER IS

In a very real sense, a storyteller, in the art of telling his tale, loses his
own personal identity. For during the telling, he has become the agent,
the go-between, through which a story gets to its audience. A good storyteller forgets himself for the time it takes to tell the story, and gives the
story a foreground. He lives in the story, and by so doing loses himself
to it.

"Imagination, perception, insight, enthusiasm, concentration are all
the qualities of any creative artist. Add to these desire to share experience
with listeners, sensitivity to the needs and moods of those listeners, sincere joy in the sharing process and you have the makings of a good storyteller," Ruth Tooze, one of America's finest storytellers today, has said.[1]

Yet it is that very personal identity which makes it possible to lose
oneself in storytelling. For it is what one brings to a story in the first

[1] Ruth Tooze, *Storytelling* (Englewood Cliffs, New Jersey: Prentice-Hall,
Inc., 1959).

This chapter is by LELAND B. JACOBS, of Teachers College, Columbia
University.

15

place that makes it possible to bring a narrative to life. The storyteller uses his distinctive talents and abilities; his background of experience in the comedy and tragedy of life; his feeling for individuals and mankind; his awareness of strong sensory impressions; his joy in language; his sensitivity to what is of spiritual and moral import; and his delight in aesthetic responses to nature and to what man has created that is beautiful. As Whitehead has pointed out, a good storyteller is an educated person, one who respects activity of thought, receptivity to beauty, humane feelings.[2] In other words, what he is by endowment and by personal cultivation gets put to use in his storytelling: his learning, his voice, his movements, his tastes and dispositions—all that gives him his unique way of coming at life.

A good storyteller is a knowing person, a wise person. A good storyteller has given himself to understanding, as well as he can, how man copes with life in its various manifestations. He understands children in their development, and their curiosities, concerns, and commitments. He gives himself to some of the arts for their insights about knowing through aesthetic responses. And he queries static or platitudinous approaches to solutions, seeking more dynamic and open ways to thinking and feeling.

All these propensities to know, to quest, to question pay dividends in his storytelling—they give it depth, and dignity, and, if one would not be misunderstood by saying so, divinity.

A good storyteller cultivates his expertness in the language. He listens to the basic rhythm patterns of spoken language, the musical lilt of language, the effectual folk expressions. He observes the word precisely used, the neat turn of phrase, the fresh figure of speech. He notes the patterning of writing, the tempo and nuances of meaning. All this he does, to the end that the language of his storytelling is used with good effect.

As the instrumentality for getting a tale well told to his audience, the storyteller is a wise and knowing individual, a dynamic alert observer, a person who delights in and uses language charmingly. He is, in sum, the kind of person with whom children ought to be associated.

HOW A STORYTELLER SELECTS HIS MATERIAL

There is no dearth of good storytelling material, though not all stories written are good for storytelling. Some are better read than told.

The story to tell to young children is one whose plot is compact, direct, and well paced, whose problem is early established, and whose resolution holds the listener to the very last word. The time and place should

---

[2] Alfred North Whitehead, *The Aims of Education* (New York: The Macmillan Company, 1929).

be self-explanatory, with just such essential details as will create enticing pictures in the mind. The characters should be few, since the young child will not be able to hold very many characters in mind. Too, the characters should be established early, and their basic behavior patterns clear, so that the listener can immediately identify with them and become in-volved in what happens to them. Also, whether the story is one of reality or fancy, "believe" or "make believe," must be established at the very beginning, and the mood developed should authentically support this reality or fancy.

Important as all these matters of choice are, more important still is that the stories one tells to children should be worth telling, over and over again. A story prepared carefully takes considerable energy. That energy should be given only to stories that are rooted in big ideas, like acceptance, affection, belonging, approval; stories that are beautifully written; stories that are in the tradition of the best literature there is to offer young children.

To find such stories, one would quite naturally turn to the literature of our heritage—the stories of talking animals, of wise and foolish fellows, of magic and preternatural creatures, of rigmarole language. Many old accumulative tales and folk and fairy tales are good choices for young children. Yet one should not use these indiscriminately, for some of them, in terms of child development, are really better suited to older children.

Of course there is also the wide range of modern children's stories from which to select, such as:

- Stories of animals, like *Millions of Cats; The Story of Ping; Make Way for Ducklings.*

- Stories of everyday experiences, like *Little Boy Brown; Rosa-Too-Little; Willie's Walk to Grandma's.*

- Stories of make-believe, like *Georgie; The Five Hundred Hats of Bartholomew Cubbins; The Five Chinese Brothers.*

- Stories of high days and holidays, like *Ask Mr. Bear; The Animals Came First; Pumpkin Moonshine.*

- Stories of far away or long ago, like *Down Down the Mountain; Mei Li; Mitty and Mr. Syrup; Crow Boy.*

- Stories of today's mechanical world, like *Mike Mulligan; Two Little Trains; The Little Old Auto; Little Toot.*

- Stories of laughter like *The Rabbit's Revenge; Smokey's Big Discovery; The Backward Day; Hundreds and Hundreds of Pancakes.*

- Stories of the great outdoors, like *Blueberries for Sal; Play with Me; The Little Island.*

One more matter has to be taken into account: one's own enthusiasm for and total enjoyment of the story. Sometimes adults think, "Children ought to hear this story; therefore I will learn to tell it." That is only the starting point. One must go further and query himself: Do I deeply appreciate this story? Does its sequence of development come quite spontaneously to mind? Do I see its pictures, its movement, feel its mood and tone and hear it naturally? Does it possess some big idea that gives it its inner strength? Do I think it beautiful? Am I satisfied with it in all its parts? Does it seem really to belong to me?

HOW A STORYTELLER PREPARES FOR THE TELLING

Having selected a story to learn to tell, the teller prepares it for telling. He observes the total patterning of the story—the keys to its unfolding. He notes the point of view from which the story is told. He gives attention to details and clues to further developments in the story that must be skillfully directed in the telling. He considers how he will handle the beginning and ending of the story. He visualizes scenes and actions and characters. All this he does to the end of absorbing the story as a totality: story line, characterization, transitions, pacing, and patterning.

Then the storyteller must decide whether he will memorize the story as written, or whether he will fix story line in his mind and tell it partially in his own words, always being sure to keep neatly turned phrases, rhymes or verses, or other such elements just as the author tells them. If the story has been selected with care, one is likely to have a goodly part of the preparation already done.

Another form of preparation is what to do about creating a background for the telling. Most stories will need little or no background laid; the teller will begin with a brief, direct statement: "Today I'll tell you a story about . . ."; "This is the story of . . ."; "Have you ever heard how . . . ?" However, on occasion, there is something sufficiently unusual in the story that it needs explanation for full enjoyment of it. In such instances, what is to precede the story needs to be planned, so that it harmonizes with the story, so that the teller can move with finesse from the introduction into the story itself. The introduction may be an explanation by the teller, a series of questions to be answered either from the audience or by the teller, or pictures or objects that further understanding.

HOW TO USE THE TELLING TIME

Once story time has come, though it may not be the most important matter, it is wise to get the group settled comfortably, with children who may disturb each other separated, the child with some hearing loss in a front position, and a sense of physical comfort and anticipation established.

With the setting taken care of, one begins, keeping eye contact, sizing up response. He observes if the voice reaches all listeners; if the tempo is about right; if he seems to be holding his audience.

As the story progresses, a child may make some comment, ask what a word means, anticipate out loud what is coming next. These, at times, can be ignored, the teller keeping the story moving, with renewed emphasis on the story itself. If the child's insistence cannot be ignored, the skillful teller often weaves the child's comment or question right into his telling, thus preserving the integrity of an unbroken story line and yet not ignoring the child.

If for some reason the telling gets too badly disrupted, by subtle intrusions, unexpected interruptions, or restlessness or uneasiness on the part of the children, it is probably wisest to acknowledge calmly that it just isn't the right time for this story, and go on to some other activity. Which does not mean that all is lost, for there undoubtedly will come a more auspicious time for sharing the story.

When a story has been told, often there is no follow-up planned at all. The responses of the children will be enough. Surely, pat remarks like "Wasn't that a nice story?" or "Did you like it?" add nothing to the telling. If the teller thinks that some discussion of the story would be appropriate, the lead questions should be more than mere recall. They should, rather, be questions that get at actual thought or total meaning, that give added insight, that make the story the more memorable.

The recompense for a story well told is great. "Tell it again," "That's a good story," "Do you know some more stories like that?" is pay enough for the effort it takes to prepare and tell a story to young children. The spontaneous laughter, the moment of absolute silence at the story's end, the immediate response, "I know a story like that"—these are big dividends, enough to send one out further to perfect his art: by self-criticism of one's accomplishments, by considering new ventures in one's tellings, by further study of story art from great storytellers themselves.

SELECTED READINGS

Ruth Sawyer, *The Way of the Storyteller*. New York: Viking Press, Inc., 1942.

Marie Shedlock, *The Art of Storytelling*. New York: Dover Publications, 1951.

Ruth Tooze, *Storytelling*. Englewood Cliffs, N. J.: Prentice-Hall, Inc., 1959.

Presenting poetry

to children

Time for poetry can be a happy part of the literature program with young children. They seem readily, almost naturally, attuned to lilting rhythm, cadenced line, well-selected phrases, graphic pictures, and movement in verse form. They respond to the immediacy and vibrancy of the poet's craft. They even quickly learn lines and verses which particularly appeal to them. When poetry is selected in terms of what they have demonstrated they enjoy, when the conditions for the sharing are comfortable both physically and psychologically, and when the reading is well done, time for poetry is surely a great moment in the day.

KNOWING MOTHER GOOSE

Mother Goose rhymes have long held an honored place in the literary heritage of young children. Moreover, there are good reasons why this has been the case. The Mother Goose rhymes are actionful. They are fast-paced, both actually and psychologically. Many are suggestive of rhythmic movement and play-acting. A goodly number tell pint-sized stories. They frequently call up distinctive pictures in the mind's eye. They often produce, in one way or another, hearty laughter. They are pleasing in their rhyming, their use of nonsense syllables, tongue-tickling expressions, onomatopoetic phrases. They are quite individual—no sameness from verse to verse can dull the senses with monotony. And they sing their way almost effortlessly into one's memory.

As one uses the Mother Goose rhymes with young children, he can, of course, just read them higgledy-piggledy. But one can also read them as groupings—as verses about boys, or girls, or "old women," or as character

This chapter is by LELAND B. JACOBS, of Teachers College, Columbia University.

sketches, little stories, riddles, gesture and action rhymes, tongue twisters, or counting-out jingles. If one reads them by such groupings, comparisons and contrasts show up and thus encourage the children to talk about them, or act them out, or respond to them in some knowing way. "The old woman in the shoe had a harder life than the old woman who lived under the hill," said a young listener. "Which Mary do you like better—the contrary one or the one who had the lamb?" asked one young miss. Groupings of the jingles can facilitate these kinds of responses.

The playing out of some of the Mother Goose rhymes can give great delight to the poetry period. "Hark, hark, the dogs do bark" may be a bit noisy but it is richly dramatic. "Jack Be Nimble" and "Little Miss Muffet" call for yet different forms of playing out. So Mother Goose provides an outlet for individual responses, parallel or small group acting, and whole group participation.

One collection of Mother Goose rhymes, good as it may be, is not enough. To have several for children to see adds a dimension through the illustrations. Different artists' conceptions of "Wee Willie Winkie" or "Jack Sprat" extend the child's imagination and open doors to aesthetic interpretations that an encounter with only one edition does not afford. And surely familiarity with the Petershams' collection of American folk rhymes, *The Rooster Crows*, should be part of children's encounters with Mother Goose.

SELECTING MODERN POETRY

One will also want to use modern poetry with young children. Of course, it must be poetry that the adult enjoys; else he will not be able to do right by the stanzas with children.

Surely one will look into A. A. Milne's poems for this age group; and there are others, among them Dorothy Aldis, Harry Behn, Kate Greenaway, Robert Louis Stevenson, Leslie Brooke, William Jay Smith, Christina Rossetti, Myra Cohn Livingston, Walter de la Mare, Aileen Fischer, James S. Tippett, Ivy O. Eastwick, and Margaret Wise Brown. But one shouldn't make the mistake of thinking it necessary to stick to "children's poetry." There are gems that even young children may mightily enjoy among the works of many highly sophisticated poets.

Moreover, in selecting poems for young children, one will want to be sure it is quite good poetry—that is, poetry which

■ *Possesses truly poetic content.*

Is the meaning an aesthetic meaning rather than a matter of ordinary discourse?

Is the total conception fresh and unhackneyed?

Is the imagery feelingfully graphic?

21

- *Uses words appropriate to the meaning to be felt.*

    Is there the feel of precise sensory impressions?

    Is the poem free from too difficult figurative or allusive language?

    Do the word combinations have freshness and originality?

    Are the images, deductions, observations presented in childlike (but not childish) language?

- *Has delightful melody and movement.*

    Is the sound appropriate to the poetic content?

    Does the sound of the lines come unaffectedly and smoothly from the reader's lips?

    Is the rhythmic pattern in keeping with the poetic content?

    Is the movement of the poem integral in the mood and meaning?

    Are the rhymings seemingly natural and unforced even if they are funny or unexpected?

When one has located those poems to which he himself responds with enthusiasm, and which he thinks are good poems to present to children, then he is ready to ask, "How shall I present them?"

USING POETRY TIME EFFECTUALLY

With young children, the poems will be presented orally by the teacher. And since oral interpretative reading is dependent not only on the oralization but on the aesthetic meaning of the poem, the latter is the next consideration. What is the poem really about? Is it a bit of delicious nonsense? Is it a precise word picture? Is it an insight into a way of reacting to something actual or tangible? Or to something tremendously important in life? Is it an appealing story? How one actually reads the stanzas grows out of what one finds in them.

Then the question is how the poem shall be read. Are there quiet lines? Loud ones? In what tempo should it be heard? Are there tripping lines? Slower ones? Is the poem to emphasize action? Picture? Meditation? In the lines themselves, the poet has given clues to possible interpretations. The reading, when sensitively done, gives clues to these possibilities which one takes advantage of in his oral presentation. Just think of how differently one should read "Jack Be Nimble," "Twinkle, Twinkle, Little Star," "The Grand Old Duke of York," and "The Three Little Kittens," and of the variety of moods and effects which should be evident to the young listeners from the reading.

When the poetry reading has been planned, one next has to decide if there is to be some introduction and some follow-up in connection with the reading. Will some comments or discussion precede the poems? If so, for what reason: To set a mood? To start a train of thought and feeling? To alert the group to a reason for listening? And when the poems have been read, will one initiate some form of follow-up, such as discussion, dramatization, or choral reading? If so, do the poems necessarily lend themselves, for further enjoyment of the stanzas, to such a follow-up? Or would it be better, with certain poems, to get the clues or leads from what the children might suggest?

Merely to ask "Did you like it?" will not suffice. A sensitive adult ought to be able to answer that without asking. Moreover, the asking has little relationship to the meaning of the poetry. This question is empty; it leads nowhere so far as true enjoyment of poetry is concerned.

CONSIDERING OTHER TEACHING SUGGESTIONS

Other suggestions for enjoying poetry with children can be proposed. For instance, one can collect and have ready for use certain poems that relate to common experiences that are likely to occur—poems to turn to quickly, on the spur of the moment. Such poems might deal with weather conditions, or daily happenings, or common sights or sounds, or play activities. Then, when the occasion seems just right for it, the teacher can bring a poem immediately to the situation, thus giving both the experience and the poem heightened meaning.

One can also develop poem cycles—groups of poems, on the same topic or theme, which when shared at one time give that focus various aesthetic interpretations. When one has several such cycles to share (on, say, clothing, counting, pets, playing, community helpers, and the like), he is extending the meaning of poetry's way of knowing. He is providing the opportunity for children to note that there are many ways to come at sensations, observations, and reactions poetically.

Recordings of poems—both spoken and sung—can be used effectually. Of course, recordings are no substitute for the adult's frequent reading to the group. But as a complement, as a way to hear poems in other voices, other interpretations, such recordings can add another dimension to the young child's experiences with poetry.

Sharing times, when each child says a poem he knows, can give the child interpreter a chance to put his repertoire to use, to feel the joy of having a listening audience, and to do interpretative, dramatic reading. The audience of listeners can hear poems they might otherwise not know, and can be involved in yet another kind of shared aesthetic experience. For the teacher, he can see reflected his own reading; he can also see the kinds of content, the kinds of appeals that "get to" children and thus be aided in his future selection of poems to read to the group.

23

From all such practices in getting children and poems together, as well as from the on-going life activities of the children, will undoubtedly come some original poetic responses from them. Poems may emerge spontaneously, in talking together, or as the child tells something. Get it—put it down on paper, to feed back to the child as original poetry-making. Or one can try, consciously, to get children to respond aesthetically to some component of living. Whichever way, to encourage poetry-making by children is to give them a vital part of their total contact with this form of literature.

With young children, memorization of lines and stanzas will come about quite naturally. When children say, enthusiastically, "Read it again," and "Again," they are coming into memorization. When the teacher asks the group what poems they would like to hear again, he is encouraging memorization. When the teacher reads a poem read previously, and invites the children to say any part that they know with him, he is leading them into memorization. When he gives them opportunities to say poems, or lines, that they have learned by heart, he is giving memorization its fulfillment.

Pleasure in poetry is not foreign to young children. When poems are given a real chance to work their spells, with the aid of a sensitive, enthusiastic adult, poetry becomes indispensable, a vibrant, life-related affirmation of joy in being, and a true clarification of the new, the wonderful, the intimate, the in-no-other-way-describable sense of things. Then there is, for the young child, what William Butler Yeats thought should come from the reading of poetry: "Blood, imagination and intellect running together."

Doing choral speaking

Choral speaking deserves a place in every primary grade classroom. No schoolchild is too young to commence choral speaking. No teacher is fundamentally incapable of helping children achieve satisfying results from choral speaking.

The term choral speaking includes the concepts of choral reading and verse choir work. Basically, it implies the employment of several voices to render, for the most part in unison, a prose or poetry selection.

The major objective of choral speaking, so far as public school classrooms are concerned, is a simple one. That objective is to *help children discover some of the delights of literature.* All choral activities which contribute to the accomplishment of this objective are worthy ones. Any choral activities which detract from the attainment of this objective should be abandoned.

VALUES OF CHORAL SPEAKING

As one works with his group toward helping children discover the delights of literature through choral speaking, there are many values which accrue to children and teacher.

A new dimension of literature is discovered. So much of the child's school time is occupied with the task of acquiring literal meaning from print that the potential beauty of the spoken word is frequently neglected. Choral speaking can help children come to the discovery that print may carry added meaning when translated into sound. Emotional undertones are revealed. The interaction of the sounds of words, one

---

This chapter is by SHELTON L. ROOT, JR., of Wayne State University, Michigan.

with another, helps build mood. In a sense, choral speaking helps literature, especially poetry, escape the confines of print which so often holds it prisoner.

The ear is "tuned" to the sound of literature. Choral speaking can help children hear their literature, even when they are reading silently to themselves. Far from always discouraging children from sub-vocalizing when they are reading silently, there are times when the full import of the printed word can be appreciated only when it is heard. In silent reading, it is the "inner ear" which must do the hearing. Choral speaking helps tune that inner ear to listen for the vocal meaning of words.

Children learn to match their voices to the feeling-tone of literature. There are few more effective ways of helping children acquire the facility of using their voices to reinforce the meaning of words than through choral speaking. As the teacher helps children interpret orally the meaning of literature, he automatically, and usually indirectly, guides children to match their voices to the spirit of the selection. As facility with choral speaking increases, children discover their ability to use their voices to greater advantage.

Every child is a part of the group effort. In choral speaking there are no voices which are unsuitable. Each child's voice contributes to the effectiveness of the presentation. Shy, self-conscious children are supported by other members of the group. The most assertive children learn self-discipline as they accept responsibility for the success of the presentation. The result is that all children acquire an increasing sense of identity with and importance to their peers.

Providing pleasure for others brings a sense of accomplishment to the participants. The major function of choral speaking is not to "show off" at school assemblies, P.T.A. meetings, and similar affairs. But there are, and should be, occasions when children choose to demonstrate their accomplishments to others. When such occasions arise, children gain satisfaction from discovering that what they have done to please themselves also pleases others.

APPROPRIATE SELECTIONS

There is some prose which lends itself to choral speaking. It can be recognized by its simplicity of syntax, its rhythmic sentence structure, and its heavy lacing with "sound" words. Actually, though written in prose form, it possesses most of the ingredients of poetry.

For the most part, poetry is the literary form best suited to choral speaking. Not all poetry is equally appropriate, however. The best selections have about them the following characteristics:

- They are strongly cadenced.
- They provide for contrasts in sound and cadence and mood.
- They are structurally uncomplicated.
- They may be either lyric or narrative, but their subject matter and its treatment is appealing to young children.
- They are usually brief enough to be rather easily memorized.
- They possess the qualities of good poetry.

GETTING STARTED

Choral speaking grows best in a classroom climate which encourages poetry in many ways. Teachers who enjoy reading poetry regularly to their classes, who put favorite poems on experience charts and display them in the room, and who encourage children to make their own poetry experience little difficulty in commencing choral speaking. They find that in this way there is already at hand a group of poems which children like and with which they are familiar. Nearly every teacher who has read poetry to children has had the experience of having them voluntarily join in on familiar passages and refrains. This is actually a natural beginning for choral speaking. It should be encouraged.

The secret of successful choral speaking lies in pleasurable beginnings. And, especially for young children, it lies in successful first attempts. Therefore, the best selections to start with are those which are already known and enjoyed by the group. In that way there is no tedious preliminary assignment of poetry to be memorized at home.

Nursery rhymes are natural starters for most young children. They are already known, are short, place few demands on those who may be learning them for the first time, and can be spoken with a happy abandon which less familiar selections would discourage.

Successful beginnings are heavily dependent upon simplicity of execution. This means that much satisfying unison work should be done before commencing more complicated work with solo and choir parts. Unison speaking keeps the weight of individual perfection from resting too heavily on the consciousness of young speakers. If one should forget a line or make a word substitution, he can continue without the embarrassment of having seriously interrupted the group effort.

27

Good direction is essential to good beginnings. One great advantage of speaking poetry which is already known, rather than reading less familiar poetry, is that children can give their undivided attention to the teacher-director. For if the speaking is ragged, drags, or is monotonously sing-songy, children will never catch the vital spark of enthusiasm.

To make the direction easiest, the teacher groups the children in a standing position where they all can see. The signal to commence should be given only after every child clearly understands what is to be done and is ready. Verbal instructions need to be kept brief and to the point. If they are not, attention wanders and interest lags.

After teacher and children have had some successes, there is a time when children may try their hands at leading the group. However, since the results are often less satisfying to the children, it is a practice which should be carefully regulated.

The most effective single means of instruction is the example set by the teacher as he leads the children. From him, children take their cues concerning phrasing, tempo, diction, and emphasis. It is he who must help the children understand that with choral speaking, every word must be clearly understandable to the listener.

MOVING ON

Once the group has had several pleasing experiences with easy unison speaking, it is ready to begin variations. There are many which add to the flexibility of choral speaking. Each has some unique advantages.

Solo parts can be identified, with the group speaking the refrain. A few poems lend themselves to each child speaking a line, again with the group speaking the refrains in chorus. Much poetry can be spoken more effectively when the group is divided into two or three choruses. If two choruses are to be used, high voices are grouped in one, low voices in the other. When three choruses are appropriate, a separate group is formed for the middle-range voices. But, for the most part, two choruses are sufficient insofar as young children are concerned. Choruses may be used to respond to one another, to speak refrains, and to provide rhythmic accompaniment.

Good examples of two-chorus selections are "Hickory, Dickory, Dock" and Vachel Lindsay's "Little Turtle." With "Hickory, Dickory, Dock," one chorus speaks the words while the other provides the accompaniment with a quietly spoken and repeated *tick tock, tick tock,* etc. With "The Little Turtle" the choruses speak alternate lines, then speak the last line in unison.

One pleasing feature of choral speaking is that children can suggest a variety of interpretations and executions. Such suggestions should be encouraged. Not only may they prove interesting to do, but the very doing helps children realize that the interpretation of poetry is, to some extent, a personal matter.

When children have mastered the mechanics of reading, a wider selection of poetry is available for choral speaking. The group's repertoire is increased by duplicating copies of many of the children's favorites, sometimes scoring them for easier reading. When poems are to be read, rather than recited from memory, it is wise to read them aloud together several times until everyone is familiar with their content. Only after such familiarization should there be any elaboration of parts.

One technique for helping groups improve their efforts is to periodically permit a few children to act as listeners. This small group removes itself from the chorus and acts as a critical audience. It praises the meritorious and makes suggestions for improvement. Another effective technique is to make occasional tape recordings so that all the children may share in the evaluation of their own efforts. Through such devices, the group is encouraged to set its own increasingly high standards. And standards are important, for the inevitable reward of slipshod work is disenchantment.

PITFALLS

Three pitfalls which need to be avoided are the use of poor selections, harsh voices, and cuteness. In the first instance, children soon tire of second-rate poetry, and its rewards are not worth the effort of mastering it. In the second instance, children's voices have a natural tendency to become harsh as excitement increases. It is up to the teacher to help children keep their voices light in order to achieve the most satisfying results. The pitfall of cuteness can be the undoing of choral speaking. It is the "dear, sweet children" approach which pleases some misguided adults, but which soon makes children aware it is they who are being put on exhibition and not their accomplishments.

SUMMARY

Choral speaking is a rewarding activity when teacher and children enter into it naturally and with the goal of enjoyment uppermost in mind, and when the teacher nurtures its growth through patient understanding and warm enthusiasm.

Relating creative experiences

to literature

Young children are uniquely equipped to experience literature creatively, and today's literature for young children has qualities that offer unique potential for its use in this way. Teachers, understanding the nature of the creativity of young children, knowing the literature, and sensitive to the nature of the setting and conditions for using it, find many ways to draw upon and nourish the creativity of young children.

THE CREATIVITY OF YOUNG CHILDREN

Young children respond spontaneously to literature. No one who has read to children needs to be told that they are whole-hearted appreciators of literature. Their faces, their bodies, and their voices all attest to a conscious sense of enjoyment and pleasure that are characteristic of creative experience. Not only do children enjoy, but they let us know about it now. The planned and ordered commentary of older groups is not for them. Experiencing literature is not a spectator sport!

Young children experience literature through all of their senses. Not only do children respond, but all sensory avenues are used in the process. Impression and expression are so intermingled that the reading of literature is likely to be interrupted by laughter, sound effects, and bodily movement. They sway to the rhythm of the language, they imitate its sounds. They giggle when it's funny, shudder when it's scary, and wiggle when it's exciting. They cover their eyes, stop their ears, hold their noses, wave their arms, and tap their feet. And sometimes they sit transfixed, conjuring up the whole scene in their minds' eyes.

This chapter is by EVELYN WENZEL, of the University of Florida.

Young children are active explorers and thinkers. They identify easily and naturally with events and people in literature. Their own experiences are available immediately to relate to what they hear. They question and comment, agree and disagree, pass judgment and predict outcomes. They are rigorous noters of detail. If illustration does not exactly match text, if detail in one part of the story contradicts that in another part, if one version departs in the slightest degree from another, the author, illustrator, or reader is reminded in short order.

This relating of their own experience with that in books may take place simultaneously as they listen or read. But it may take place tomorrow, next week, or next month. One mother, puzzled by hearing her four-year-old in his bath one night repeating over and over, "Tut, tut, it looks like rain," had forgotten the Pooh story read a week before. But he hadn't! This ability to collect experience and draw upon it at some future time is an important ingredient of all creative effort.

LITERATURE FOR CREATIVE EXPERIENCES

Literature can invite spontaneous participation. Since much of the experience of literature comes to young children as adults read to them, such literature should be fun to read aloud, as well as fun to listen to, and should provide many opportunities for children to participate spontaneously.

Good read-aloud books hold up well after repeated readings because the meaning and the "feel" of the meaning are communicated as much by the rhythm of the language as by the meaning of the words:

> Up from the floor of the barn rose the cages, rows and rows of cages, cages above cages—floor-low and man-high. And in each cage—floor-low, man-high was a barking dog.[1]

The combination of rhythm and repetition of sound effects, words, phrases, and sentences invites participation as children hear favorite stories and poems read and reread. Some such parts of stories have been repeated by generations of children; others are from books with the ink, as yet, hardly dry:

And it came to pass in those days . . .

"TRIP, TRAP! TRIP, TRAP! TRIP, TRAP!" went the bridge.
"Who's that tripping over my bridge?"

Mirror, mirror, on the wall,
Who is the fairest of them all?

[1] From *The Last Little Cat,* by Meindert De Jong. New York: Harper, 1961.

. . . the great, grey-green greasy Limpopo River, all set about with fever trees. . . .[2]

> Cats here, cats there,
> Cats and kittens everywhere,
> Hundreds of cats,
> Thousands of cats,
> Millions and billions and trillions of cats.[3]

But Grandfather and I
never hurry.
We walk along,
and walk along
And stop . . . and look . . . just as long as we like.[4]

Oh, he walked around the world
on his four fur feet,
his four fur feet,
his four fur feet.
And he walked around the world
on his four fur feet
and never made a sound—O.[5]

Thus does the language of literature—both great and less great—take firm hold on memory at an age when remembering is an effortless pleasure.

Literature can enrich sensory experiences. The ready blending of direct and vicarious experiences is nowhere more evident than in watching children enjoy the sensory experiences that literature provides in such variety: feeling with The Elephant's Child the "cool, schloopy, sloshy mud-cap all trickly behind his ears"; tasting pancakes that were "feathery, fluffy, and flavory, tender and toothsome, incredibly savory"; [6] seeing with Rim the world from high up on a horse (in *Angus and the Ducks,* by Marjorie Flack); touching the Clare Newberry cats; pointing out,

---

[2] From "The Elephant's Child," in *Just So Stories,* by Rudyard Kipling. New York: Doubleday, 1902.

[3] From *Millions of Cats,* by Wanda Gág. New York: Coward-McCann, 1928. Copyright 1928 by Coward-McCann, Inc.

[4] From *Grandfather and I,* by Helen Buckley. Copyright 1959 by Lothrop, Lee & Shepard Co., Inc.

[5] From *Four Fur Feet,* by Margaret Wise Brown. Copyright 1961 by the publisher. Permission granted by the publisher, William R. Scott, Inc.

[6] From *The Perfect Pancake,* by Virginia Kahl. New York: Scribner, 1960.

object by object, the changing details of the pictures in *The Little House* (Burton); hearing mouth-filling, tongue-twisting words that are so conspicuously absent from the books children read for themselves in their early school years. There are "James James / Morrison Morrison / Weatherby George Dupree"; [7] and "Madeleine, Gwendolyn, Jane and Clothilde, / Caroline, Genevieve, Maude, and Mathilde, / Willibald, Guinevere, Joan and Brunhilde, / And the youngest of all . . . the baby, Gunhilde," whose mother set out to bake "a lovely light luscious delectable cake." [8]

Literature opens doors for thinking and feeling. The experience of standing in someone else's shoes, of seeing the world through his eyes, is truly a creative one. Children who know what it is like to do everything wrong, to be scolded for getting into things, to be told to hurry, hurry, hurry, or to have a very special grown-up at just the right time, can get special enjoyment from *Lucky McLockett* (McGinley), *Angus and the Ducks* or *Wait for William* (Flack), and *Grandfather and I* or *Grandmother and I* (Buckley).

John Ciardi has said that "Art is the way the mind breathes; [that literature is a form of art where the reader can find] the center of value, uncluttered by peripheral confusions." [9] The best literature for young children says something important about life. It is a potent means of communicating values that have evolved out of the long struggle of the race to become civilized. The folk tales for young children do this, perhaps in the most "uncluttered" form, but so do many of the simplest picture books. Children may somehow learn about the dignity of work in *Mike Mulligan and His Steam Shovel* (Burton); about the limitations of the accelerated pace of modern living in *Grandfather and I;* and about the security of life going on from one day to the next among familiar and beloved surroundings in *Good Night, Mr. Beetle* (Jacobs).

We see and hear children respond to the story, to the pictures, and to the language, but seldom, if ever, to the value-content of literature. For the uniqueness of literature's "teaching" lies in its subtleness. We may catch a glimmer eventually and indirectly, but its message can never be forced by moralizing.

[7] From *When We Were Very Young*, by A. A. Milne. Copyright, 1924, renewal, 1952 by A. A. Milne. Reprinted by permission of E. P. Dutton & Co., Inc.

[8] From *The Duchess Bakes a Cake*, by Virginia Kahl. New York: Scribner, 1955.

[9] "Literature Undefended." Editorial, *Saturday Review*, 42 (January 31, 1959), p. 22.

THE SETTING FOR CREATIVE EXPERIENCES

Young children should be close to the reader and to the books so that the softly spoken as well as the shouted reaction can be heard; so that pictures and words can be seen and pointed to; so that the warm closeness of others enjoying the same story will be associated with books and reading together.

Books should be easily accessible to everyone. Teachers find even the school library too far away when the moment is just right for a story or a poem. A few choice collections of stories and poems, as well as a few perennial favorite books, are essential on a teacher's desk.

Children need books to hold, to feel, and to browse through at leisure. After a story is read, the book should be left around for individuals and small groups to look at and talk over. Older children, reading on their own, need books of all kinds on shelves, tables, and in their own private storage spots. The school library should be available to all age groups.

Young children need time to enjoy and respond to literature—to say the words, to make the sound effects, to ask questions, to make comments: "Once I had a rabbit . . . ." "My daddy says . . . ." "What's 'invisible'?" "Why did he do that?" "That's not what I'd do." Thus children relate and explore; thus a teacher learns about their understandings and misunderstandings; thus literature, in its own time, carries its message.

Materials of many kinds should be at hand. Young children need avenues in addition to verbal ones to tell about their experiences with literature—art materials of all kinds to tell stories or to depict favorite parts; costumes and properties for dramatic play and dramatizations, sometimes spontaneous, sometimes planned; paper for writing their own stories after they pass the dictation-to-teacher stage; a puppet stage and some "general purpose" puppets that can be put to quick use for reproducing stories or creating ones of their own. (The same puppet can become, with a few minor adjustments, a mother, a fairy godmother, or a witch.)

Filmstrips, such as the ones from the Weston Wood Studios, make illustrations equally visible to everyone. They provide, also, opportunities for children to retell favorite stories in their own words. They suggest, too, a way of putting children's own pictures together to tell stories.

Out of books creatively experienced in early childhood emerge the most permanent memories of later years. Somehow no version of Cinderella is quite satisfying if it is other than the first one experienced, and the most beautiful of modern illustrations of Mother Goose may disappoint the grown-up who carries in his mind's eye the pictures in the battered edition of his early childhood. But stories and pictures are not all. The feel and smell of books and libraries, the experience of closeness to some beloved storyteller and to others sharing the same experience, and perhaps a movie or television version of a favorite story—all may be part of the grown-up's memory of childhood literature experience. What he probably cannot remember acquiring at all—the ideas, values, and knowledge that have become a part of him—may be the most important contribution of literature to his living.

Dramatizing literature

with young children

Dramatizing literature gives children an opportunity to get behind printed words, closer to the reality that forced these words to be written. In assuming the role of another person, by forming movements or expressing sounds found in this reality, the participants experience another way of knowing literature.

In the earliest school years the teacher reads much literature with dramatic potentiality, but does not directly guide dramatic activities. The children, without direction, often dramatize a story or poem during their play. This dramatic play, stimulated by the reading, is their way of capturing the dramatic quality of the literature, of making drama.

Beginning in the kindergarten and continuing throughout the remaining school years, creative dramatics, guided by the teacher, is possible. This art form can take place in any classroom, since it requires no special costumes, props, or scenery, but only a teacher, a group of children, and a story or poem. Under the guidance of the teacher, the children, portraying characters or movements evoked by the story or poem, step into a specific dramatic setting and cause the author's words to become reality. The participants, acting out a piece of literature according to their comprehension of it, create an emerging drama.

Three kinds of literature with dramatic potential can be read to young children for dramatization:

■ Materials with a definite plot, characters, actions, and dialogue.

■ Literature involving only characters and action.

■ Selections that, through the careful choice and placement of words, present only movement, rhythm, sound, and color.

This chapter is by WANNA ZINSMASTER, of Los Angeles State College.
36

The first consideration for the dramatization of any literature is simplicity: an uncomplicated plot, action, and characterization. The young child is yet unable to dramatize subtleties or complexities of life situations. His own forthrightness of action and characterization must also be present in the literature to be dramatized.

Since the literature is the primary fabric out of which the children will create the emerging drama, it must be of interest and concern to the children and also suggest strong leads to characterization, action, and mood. The children must be able to catch hold of forcefully descriptive words that will stimulate them to envision a specific setting and the inherent actions, dialogue, and characterizations.

If the suitability of a selection for dramatization is doubtful, a teacher can seek clues by reading it to the children. During the reading the teacher can watch for external clues from the children that may indicate their interest and involvement: facial expressions, verbal explanations, physical movements, and their reactions after the story is finished.

Not only the children must be considered in the choice of material, but also the teacher's own feelings and thoughts about a story or poem. If a teacher finds it difficult to appreciate or read a particular kind of literature, he must not consider it for dramatization. The teacher, like the child, must to some extent feel involved with the action, mood, and people of the selection. He cannot guide children to create dialogue and action from literature if he does not have some empathetic feeling for the content and at least some imagination of the possible original reality.

Sometimes an entire selection can be dramatized, but in some instances the complexity or length of a selection may demand the dramatization of only a section. The teacher, knowing the children, during his own preparation can surmise parts that the children would be likely to dramatize. Later, as he reads or tells the selection to the children, he can note the sections that seem to appeal particularly to the children and seek their suggestions.

HOW DOES A TEACHER PREPARE?

The teacher during this preparation must come to know intimately the story or poem chosen for dramatization. He seeks to make the content come alive by reading and re-reading in a way that permits him to envision possible thoughts, feelings, movements, and sounds inherent in the selection. The teacher asks himself:

- How do these people feel?
- What are they doing or thinking?
- How do they move?

- What do they look like?

- Why do they act as they do?

- What is happening in this particular setting?

If the story or poem is without specific characters, the teacher can seek to discern the rhythm, sounds, and movements evoked by the author's words and ask:

- What kinds of movement and sound do these words suggest?

- How can these movements be shown?

- How can the suggested sounds be made?

- What parts of the body can be used?

Questions concerning thoughts, feelings, and movements can help the teacher begin to bring into existence living characters engaged in real actions; to create sounds and movements visibly and audibly.

Instead of answering the questions mentally, some teachers may desire to actually experiment doing the answers; to do the movements and sounds, or to create the characterizations that the selection seems to provoke. The actual "doing" by the teacher is helpful preparation, but not essential. The teacher from his questioning and "doing" discovers hints for initiating the dramatic activity. These ideas might be written down. With these notes close at hand, the teacher knows that some ideas for dramatization already exist. These notations may also serve to spark the children's own imagination and help them see further possibilities for dramatization.

During the preparation the teacher also asks himself: "In what ways can I encourage the children to participate in creative dramatics and still feel comfortably in control of the group? Can I guide the activity more easily by directly participating in the dramatization or from the sidelines?" A teacher must begin to dramatize literature in a way in which he feels at ease and in control.

In the preparation the children are considered also: "How will they be more at ease participating—in one group, in small groups, or as individuals? In the beginning will they participate more easily by remaining seated?"

From careful preparation, the teacher can feel somewhat confident since he has become well acquainted with the literature, developed possible initiating ideas, and has clues as to how he can encourage participation by the children.

BEGINNING DRAMATIZATION

First attempts in creative dramatics should be simple and uncomplicated in order that the teacher and children can become acquainted with this art medium. A teacher can begin by having the children show familiar actions found in their daily living: eating an ice-cream cone, throwing a ball, walking through mud, or eating an apple. Later the children will begin to add words to their actions. These simple beginning experiences will help the teacher and children to move more easily into the dramatization of literature.

In preparing for a creative-dramatics session the teacher seeks to help the children to know the selection intimately by leading a discussion to the possible thoughts, feelings, and actions in the selection. Subsequently he asks the children to show these first by actions and later by actions and words. The teacher remembers during this discussion period that ideas are not always created quickly and allows time for creation: time for the mind to wonder and imagine. He is not afraid of moments of silence.

The first attempts in dramatization, as in any new activity, may appear crude and indefinite. During these beginning stages the teacher accepts the rough initial attempts of the children and finds a time to praise each child for his sincere efforts. Praise and acceptance are never forgotten by the teacher in creative dramatics.

As the children and teacher continue experimenting with creative dramatics, their dramatizations will grow in believability. The continuity of the scenes and dialogue, the characterizations and actions will become more convincing. The teacher will gain confidence in his guidance of this activity, his participation, his freedom of experimentation, and his permissiveness of movements by the children. The procedures will begin to vary and a group or groups of children may go to another part of the room to prepare dramatizations of different parts of a story or poem. During such planning periods, the teacher can move from group to group and guide the children in their own thinking and planning for their presentations.

IF THE DRAMATIZATION SEEMS TO FALTER . . .?

If the action or dialogue of a scene appears to falter, a teacher can seek to advance the dramatization by the interjection of appropriate questions or statements. This can be done either from the sidelines or by direct participation in the scene. However the teacher decides to further the scene, it is always done as part of the emerging dialogue or action. He will make his comment or suggested movement in the mood or characterization appropriate to the particular setting. If a teacher participates directly in the scene with the children he must be prepared for the children's rather pointed remarks about his participation. Many children have not seen a teacher take part in sports, art, or dramatization and are surprised that a teacher can do these things.

EVALUATION

As the children develop in dramatization they will begin to comment on the scenes and become aware of factors that make a presentation seem "real." The evaluation is guided by the teacher who, by his own attitude and comments, discourages silly or petty remarks. Evaluation includes both suggestions for improvement and acknowledgments of strengths in the dramatization. Too many suggestive comments for improvement cannot be of value until the teacher and children have developed some confidence and ease in working with this art form. The teacher must sense how many suggestions each child is ready to take and how he will profit from them. Too, the children must have the right to reject or modify proposed changes.

In dramatization of literature the teacher knows the material intimately, envisions possibilities for dramatization, determines the ways in which he and the children will participate and brings life to the content through questioning and discussion. He stimulates and guides the dramatization and leads the evaluation in a way that develops greater effectiveness in creative dramatics. Above all, he accepts every sincere effort of each child and finds a time for praise.

Enjoying literature visually

In its broadest sense, all literature is *seen*—not necessarily with the eye, but through the thought processes which provide mental meeting places for authors and children, places where ideas and relationships are seen: *visualized*.

When *enjoyment* becomes the primary purpose for providing literature experiences for boys and girls, ways will be found to allow them to think and view things in their own ways. Such ways, necessarily, will include helping children get behind and beyond the mere physical taking-in of word and picture symbols.

Literature for children is created for large audiences of boys and girls whose experiences are as varied as their interests. It is written by authors and artists whose childhood experiences generally have occurred in other times, other places.

Writers know that words summon different interpretations in different readers. They are aware that readers can be *oriented towards* their way of seeing, but they know also that readers must construct their own visual images, bring their own feelings into play, abstract their own concepts from the printed page. Writers find words convenient and necessary ways to *establish contact* with their readers, but they know also that words are just signs and symbols, arbitrarily designed and used by man to give meaning to the ideas and feelings he wishes to "picture" effectively to others. The success of this word contact which writers achieve with their readers depends upon the *visual impression* they help readers re-create for themselves, although they know too that "writing it down" can be only an approximation of the pictorial images they are calling upon readers to see.

This chapter is by CHARLES F. REASONER, of Queens College, New York.

Since individuals reconstruct their own images from the printed page in light of their unique experiences, it is important that boys and girls find *security and confidence in their discovery of personal meanings* from their reading of literature. When young children are helped to realize such discrimination in their literature experiences, it is significant to note that personal understandings are derived not only from the author's carefully-chosen words, but also from the aesthetic meanings which are *cued* by the artist. It seems essential, therefore, that boys and girls have many opportunities to extend their enjoyment of literature through various visual media.

PICTURE CUES

Just as the writer points the way with words, the illustrator also uses his art to direct the reader's interaction with literature by citing picture relationships and instances which afford him still further opportunity to build extraordinary perceptions out of ordinary meanings. As in *Raindrop Splash*, while the ordinary is present in the evaporation-condensation cycle of a drop of rain, how easy it might be for some child to dam the river, build a power plant, and light a whole town—perceiving the extraordinary from the uncontrived simplicity of the raindrops as drawn by Leonard Weisgard.

Effective use of illustration brings enjoyment to young children when they can take *additional* meanings—picture meanings—along with their experiencing of new ideas, feelings, and information they find in the printed text. These visual cues do not present the story with all the exactness and finality implied, for example, in the photograph where one feels the picture to be a "real" extension of one's own eyesight. The truly great illustrator of children's books does not ask the reader to choose between his way of interpreting the story or no way at all; neither does he do *all* the visualizing *for* the the young child. Rather he helps the reader, who is sometimes inexperienced with words or short on experience, to "dress up" old concepts or to define for himself clearer, more precise mental images of new ideas. Through similarity and contrast, for example, *size concepts* are sharply drawn by Lionni in *Inch by Inch* and by Ward in *The Little Red Lighthouse and the Great Gray Bridge.* Or, through the use of *color*, artists help the young reader experience new *aesthetic experiences* such as the changing of the seasons in Burton's *The Little House.* Or, through picture cues, perhaps the child is led to see—with greater understanding than otherwise might have been possible —the shape of a beetle; the passing of time; the differences in custom and mores of people near and far; the commonality of the hopes and problems of mankind; the degree of seriousness, gaiety, or excitement of mood implicit in the story; or an indication of whether the setting is in the real world of fact or the mental realm of fancy.

The children's artist of stature works close to the child's way of seeing; he helps children touch parts of life with their own eyes. Through the artist's work, new pathways are opened up for children's enjoyment of literature because they become more acutely aware of the *relationships* between new literature experiences and the real or imagined experiences of the past.

Although both the author and the illustrator are fundamental to the initial composition of a picture-story book, young children's enjoyment of literature often is broadened and deepened to *dimensions beyond the book* itself through visual interpretations which are made by *others* who desire to share literature with children. Some of these interpretations include the production and use of films, filmstrips, slides, and other projections, as well as puppets, "roller movies," mounted pictures, paper cutouts, and the flannel board—each of which will be discussed briefly here.

EXTENDING ENJOYMENT TO BEYOND-THE-BOOK DIMENSIONS

Statements are heard often which tend to pit one means of literature appreciation against another—statements which attempt to compare the "betterness" of stories presented in the film medium, for example, over those told with a flannel board or through the voices of puppet characters. Arguments of this kind serve only to narrow, to restrict, and to confine the wider and deeper goals of literature enjoyment—goals which include developing the *creative imagination* of children by providing them with multiple interpretations of their literature with the aid of multisensory media in variety and abundance.

There is, however, nothing inherent in moving pictures, no magic in "roller movies" or shadow puppets, which can transform a story that is ordinary or trite into an experience that is beautiful and memorable. Children are imitators; they learn by example as well as by precept. When one chooses for boys and girls visual excursions into literature which are based on the *quality of the selection* as well as on the *appropriateness of the medium* best suited for taking them into new dimensions of aesthetic appreciation and intellectual growth, it should be recognized that one also has discovered another significant way to help children develop discriminating tastes in the literature which, if not now, then eventually they will select for themselves.

Projections. Motion pictures, slides, filmstrips, overhead, opaque, and glass-slide lantern projections—when carefully selected, well prepared, and wisely used—provide additional impetus for children's enjoyment of literature. From that point in history when man first used shadows cast by sun or fire to tell and record his "time stories," young boys and girls have found enjoyment from projected still and moving-picture images.

- *Motion pictures,* traditionally, have been commercially produced and made available for children's viewing for the purposes of affording opportunities to experience not only a different story version, but also an interpretation which enhances perception of the *motion* and *action* taking place in the word and picture cues of the writer and artist.

  Puss In Boots (Encyclopaedia Britannica Films) is a good example to cite because the cat, who has many human attributes, remains true to his species in the believable "cat way" he *moves* on the screen. In addition, the swiftness with which Puss In Boots must move to keep in front of the Duke's coach—as well as the magic which enables the Ogre to change from an elephant to a mouse at will—are particular facets of the story which can be underscored by the motion-picture camera.

- *The Iconographic motion picture film* (Weston Wood Studios) is an illusion-of-motion picture growing in popularity because, in addition to photographing the original book illustrations with unique camera techniques, it also blends together sound effects and original musical scores, and utilizes the original storybook text as well. The combined result brings a delightfully different dimension to the enjoyment of a familiar tale. Robert Bright's *Georgie,* for example, provides the viewer with "something extra" when he participates in Georgie's apphehension about deciding whether or not to live in Mr. Gloam's house. The Iconographic motion picture accomplishes this through a series of "looks" exchanged between Georgie and a large portrait of Mr. Gloam.

- *"Do-it-yourself" motion picture photography* has become increasingly less expensive and technically complex. Although commercially produced motion picture films will continue to be used, it is exciting to speculate on the possibility of laymen capturing children's dramatized versions of well-loved stories on film.

- *Slides and filmstrips.* Whether the story is recorded on a strip of film or on photographic slides (either with or without sound synchronization), children find enjoyment in the total effect produced by skillful photography and expert selection and sequential arrangement of story incidents.

  In addition, boys and girls appreciate the luxury of being able to view and interact with a story, retold on slide or filmstrip, alone or with a small group of friends in a private corner of a room. Some children will find it satisfying to compare, simultaneously, the projected medium interpretation of a story with the story contained in the book. Slides and filmstrips permit one to linger as long as one wishes with a particular character or incident in a story, whether to become more familiar with a new person or idea or simply to take sheer delight in living with a favorite story character or situation for a period determined by individual interest. Others might find slides and filmstrips advantageous because they permit one to go back and refer to parts—to certain ideas—over and over again. Due to the relatively inexpensive feature of slides and filmstrips, still other children benefit from the wide range of diversified titles or different versions centering around a specific interest theme.

■ *Self-made glass slides* for "magic lantern" projections, while offering benefits very similar to those noted above, also afford creative opportunities for individuals to re-create a story experience which takes them, as well as those with whom it is shared, to yet other dimensions in literature enjoyment.

■ *Opaque projections* make it possible to project the actual illustrations of the book onto a screen. This technique might afford distinct advantages when reading or telling a story which offers a single illustration to complement many lines or pages of print. The D'Aulaires' biographies of famous Americans suggest this possibility, as does the artistry of Newberry in *April's Kittens* and of Edmonds in *The Matchlock Gun.*

The opaque projector has also been used most effectively with pictures which have been cut from magazines, calendars, and the like and mounted on cardboard. Margaret Wise Brown's story of *The House of 100 Windows,* when retold in this manner, extends the visual enjoyment of the tale not only to the cat, but to all who desire to look through the windows.

■ *The overhead projector,* still a luxury as far as the audio-visual equipment budgets of many elementary schools are concerned, opens up new frontiers for presenting different dimensions of literature experience to children. The cumulative effects of tales such as *The Old Woman and Her Pig,* Donna Hill's *Not One More Day,* and Dr. Seuss' *And to Think that I Saw It on Mulberry Street* can be collected with the technique of laying one transparency over another as the story builds and winds itself up.

Puppets.   Puppets have been constructed from materials of almost every conceivable substance: from paper clips and empty wooden spools to fresh vegetables and peanut shells! But they are brought to life by children! This flexibility in materials is matched only by versatility in type of puppet used. Paper bag puppets, finger puppets, shadow puppets, sock puppets, stick puppets, and papier-maché puppets, although they represent some of the most commonly used types, suggest only a few of the many possibilities for this kind of visual adventure.

Puppets provide visual stimuli, not so much to delineate the precise physical features of the story's main characters, but to assist in one's *involvement* with the people and circumstances of the storybook tale. Through the puppet characters' voices, dress, and mannerisms, one is helped to get into the scene and mood of the story.

45

Stories selected to be enjoyed in this medium need to be those which can depend upon the conversation of the puppet with the audience or other puppet characters (or between the puppet and the storyteller) to reveal the action, mood, scene, plot, and so forth. Marcia Brown's *Stone Soup*, for example, can be told effectively through a puppet of one of the three soldiers or from the "puppet point-of-view" of one of the towns-people. Similarly, the story of *The Three Pigs* or *The Three Billy Goats Gruff* tempts one to try new interpretations—perhaps giving the wolf's or the Troll's side of the story—via puppet characters. Esphyr Slobod-kina's *Caps for Sale* likewise can present additional pleasure when the tale is related through a conversation between the storyteller and the peddler. Or (Why not?) between the storyteller and one of the monkeys!

The flannel board. The unique visual dimension which is contributed by the flannel board to the beyond-the-book enjoyment of literature is that a continual visual interpretation of the story is built up as character by character, scene by scene, illustrations are added to and taken from the board by the storyteller.

Some stories have an *additive quality:* That is, they are tales which lead to and naturally build towards a climax as objects and characters continually "enter the picture" formed both on the board and in the young child's mind. In addition, stories best suited to the flannel board are those which have relatively simple settings, uncomplicated plots, few characters, and require little or no movement of the characters or "props." Flack's *Ask Mr. Bear*, Tworkov's *The Camel Who Took a Walk*, Weisgard's *Whose Little Bird Am I?* and Seuss' *Thidwick, the Big-Hearted Moose* are examples which offer potentials for unlimited visual interpretation.

The "roller movie." The "roller movie" is storytelling's player piano! The visual interpretations of the story, which have been "pre-recorded" on a long roll of paper, are rolled continuously past an opening for viewing. When a piece of literature is carefully selected for telling in this medium, the dimension of enjoyment significant to note is that which creates a feeling of continual, uninterrupted movement; movement which enables one to walk with Crockett Johnson's *Harold and the Purple Crayon*, with Ellis Credle's Hetty and Hank as they go *Down Down the Mountain*, or to help chase Rex Parkin's *Red Carpet*.

Paper cut-outs. The simultaneous cutting and telling of stories not only fascinates audiences, but also acquaints them with the storyteller's visual interpretation of the major objects, characters, and aspects of the scene needed to set the mood and tone of the story.

As the story is told in this paper-cutting medium, enjoyment results as much from the storyteller's imaginative manipulation of scissors as he cuts pertinent story elements from a supply of paper at his fingertips as it does from the visual images which result from the cutting and which suggest mental "taking-off" places for further excursions in literature. Once the illustration has been cut, it may be put aside while the storyteller begins on the next, or it may be displayed quickly and easily on the chalkboard or table edge with previously prepared rings of masking tape.

With only a little practice in cutting a few basic shapes (a man, woman, house, barn, hat, cat, owl, dog, monkey, and some barnyard animals) from a folded piece of construction paper, one will find his imagination and "daring" the only limiting factors to extending visual enjoyment of literature in this novel way. *The Gingerbread Boy,* Benjamin Elkin's *Six Foolish Fishermen,* and Marcia Brown's *Once A Mouse* provide this kind of visual enjoyment.

CONCLUSION

Young children live with their literature on visual frontiers created for them by authors and artists of insight and wisdom. Through word-and-picture accounts of arresting segments of life, they help boys and girls find book ways to frontier explorations of literature meanings. Although writers and illustrators can lead young people to the frontier's edge, it is here that they part, for each child must experience for himself. Each must sense and find and formulate his own concepts in the pattern presented him.

As one prepares to mediate between the young child and his literature, two concerns come immediately to mind. The first urges one to employ all the *sensitivity* at his command to insure high complementation in the selection of the story and the visual medium for extending the child's experience of the story.

The second concern urges one to take every precaution to retain the *freedom* which the children's artist achieves in his illustrations—a freedom which allows the individual to find his own way through picture and print, to come away from the literature experience with his own interpretation and enjoyment of the story.

The life the young child sees and lives is not one with a definite purpose for tomorrow but, rather, one which is rich and full of the "stuff of tomorrow"—the sense and nonsense experiences of the moment. So many of these experiences are at his fingertips—between and beyond the covers of his books.

Relating literature

to other school learnings

Changing patterns of life, the need to learn more about people and places, a growing knowledge of learning and the learner, all have led to a reappraisal of the contents of the curriculum and the teaching-learning materials for the young child. The single text devoting a section to "People Who Help Us" and another to "Neighbors Around the World" no longer satisfies the curious young reader. It does not begin to answer his questions or help him solve his problems of relationships and values. He seeks accurate and specific information but he is also concerned with attitudes and beliefs. He needs help from many sources as he attempts to "read" his ever expanding life space. While he gains facts and understandings through firsthand experience, books continue to represent the major source of his information.

CHILDREN'S LITERATURE AS A WAY OF LEARNING

Distinguished picture-story books and good books of fiction and fact have become a significant way of knowing or learning about oneself and others. They are instruments for transmitting the mores of the culture and for inculcating attitudes and values. Through books, the child experiences the common emotions of the human family. The common language of behavior of children everywhere is empathized as the young reader moves through an interesting story. The child's natural curiosity is both extended and satisfied; his interests and concerns are nurtured in the factual, realistic, and imaginative literature available today. Fortunately, the content areas of the curriculum are increasingly represented in these books. Teachers and children are gratefully turning toward them.

This chapter is by FERNE SHIPLEY of Kent State University, Ohio.

LITERATURE AIDS SOCIAL LIVING AND LEARNING

■ Books provide the child with opportunities to learn the language, thus freeing him to explore its meaning and requiring him to use his higher mental processes. The processes of thinking, perceiving, remembering, forming concepts, generalizing, and abstracting are made possible as the child acquires his vocabulary.

In order to develop his mental capacities, the child needs time to listen to stories and to study the illustrations, time to relate his own versions of them, time to ask questions and ponder about meanings, and time to use his growing vocabularly in other ways satisfying to him.

■ Distinguished literature sustains and reinforces the developing personality. The growing child is confronted with a succession of personal-social conflicts, many of which he must resolve for himself.

Through listening and reading, and through discussions in a warm, accepting environment, he is often able to gain insight into his own behavior and growth. As good feelings and confidence in himself and others accrue, he is freer to use his own potentialities.

■ First days of school are often confusing and tiring to children. Part of the problem is the result of the promise of all that school is supposed to be, along with the child's feeling of what school is. The wise teacher plans to use time and materials in ways to help children make this transition as they are able to do so. There are many ways in which books can help this process.

Books which invite looking because they are about familiar places and things are put in easily accessible places and shared with children at selected times. *Grandfather and I* (Buckley) and McCloskey's *One Morning in Maine* are representative of the good stories that help the child internalize his experiences and move toward socialization.

Books about pets and animal friends bring new learnings, but also help the child appraise what he already knows and can share with his new friends. Examples include the Angus stories by Flack, the Newberry cat stories, *The Biggest Bear* (Ward), and *Katy No-Pocket* (Payne).

Family stories help the child appreciate his own family and enable him to be articulate about its members and their activities. Berman's *When You Were a Little Baby* is especially fine for the nursery-kindergarten child who has a new brother or sister. *Wait for William* (Flack) and *The Very Little Girl* (Krasilovsky) are family stories with which children often identify. Home and family are closer, when the child can think and talk about them.

Books on subjects of particular interest to a young child lure him to new looking and reading. *What's Inside of Engines?* and *Frogs and Toads* are good examples.

LITERATURE CONTRIBUTES TO SPECIFIC CURRICULUM AREAS

■ Books help the child understand his physical environment. They supply needed information and stimulate experimentation and scientific inquiry. They provide material through which problem-solving skills are nurtured and curiosity is challenged.

Well-illustrated informational books supply accurate, detailed facts in diagrams, maps, charts, and photographs, thus clarifying and extending the language of the book. *The True Book Series* published by Children's Press is representative of this kind of material.

Well-written, "scrupulously" accurate books widen the child's vista of the world and bring him an understanding of its beauty and its secrets. *Play With Me* (Ets) is enjoyed again and again by the younger child, and children of many ages pore over books such as Hutchinson's *A Child's Book of Sea Shells.*

Concept formation, a major task of young children, is aided through well-selected materials. Time and space concepts—both personal and abstract—and cause-effect relationships may be better understood as the child examines information in Weber's *Bits That Grow Big*, Meyer's *Picture Book of the Earth*, Podendorf's *True Book of Space*, and DeRegnier's *The Shadow Book.*

Books acquaint the child with the earth's features, climate, and resources. They invite him to explore its plants and soil, and to locate himself in its realm. *What Is the World?* (Miles) and *I Live in So Many Places* (Hengesbaugh) are helpful, as is McCloskey's *Time of Wonder.*

■ Books help children get to know people and places in their world. They let him see how man adjusts to his human environment and to the cultural influences within it. They further his awareness of man's interdependence in the production of material needs and services, and contribute to his understanding of the common needs of all peoples.

Young children are busy with the problem of understanding how the work of the world goes on. Literature continues to make an excellent contribution to the child's need to know the specifics of the occupations of people. Lenski, in *Little Farm* and *Cowboy Small*, gives uncomplicated and matter-of-fact answers to the very young. *Johnny Wants to Be a Policeman* (Granberg), *The Skyscraper* (Liang), and *The First Book of Supermarkets* are representative of well-written and well-illustrated books for children in the primary grades.

Children are traveling earlier and farther and on more varied kinds of vehicles than ever before. Books and other printed materials provide much needed information and interpretation. Excellent books about cars, boats, trains, planes, and other modes of travel are available. Books similar to Golden MacDonald's *The Little Island* and Sasek's *This is Paris* tell facts about places.

The procurement of food, clothing, and shelter occupies much of man's time. Studies of these areas are an important part of the curriculum of the school and are aided by a growing number of fine books. Miles' *A House for Everyone* and the Norlings' *Pogo's Lamb* are examples.

Realistic fiction and information books teach the child about people and places in his own country and abroad. They contribute to the development of judgment and perception and furnish the context for generalizations. Lenski's *We Live by the River* and Tensen's *Come to the City* describe different kinds of life in the United States. Edel in *The Story of People* tells how much alike all people are. The Silver Burdett book *Homes Around the World* is excellent.

The past is a part of the living heritage of each child. Young children question the past and need accurate information to counteract mistaken ideas and misconceptions. The attractive picture biography *The Columbus Story*, by Dalgliesh, gives needed facts about this important man and event in our history. Kay's *Lincoln: A Big Man* helps children gain insight into the character of this national figure. Books of this stature give the child the spirit of other times and enrich his comprehension of the past.

Holiday stories and stories for special days have provided the means for preserving much of the cultural and religious heritage of various groups of people. Teachers need not and should not use the trivial in stories or poetry because there is a growing amount of quality material. Among these are the increasing numbers of good holiday story collections. Some of these also contain information about holidays in other countries.

■ While formal instruction in numbers has changed considerably in the last decade, young children have continued to use numbers functionally in their own ways. A variety of good books supply number-related experiences.

Non-numerical, quantitative concepts of size, length, and value are developing during the child's early school years. Baer's *Now This—Now That* and Berkley's *Big and Little—Up and Down* invite interesting and varied participation.

Counting books suggest natural activities such as identifying like things, enumerating and grouping, adding and taking away. These activities are often enmeshed in the joy of saying the number jingles aloud to an interested listener. Several of the Mother Goose rhymes are counting jingles as well. Françoise's book, *Jeanne Marie Counts Her Sheep*, and Watson's *What Is One?* are stories which add meaning to numbers.

THE MISUSE OF LITERATURE IN THE CURRICULUM

Literature is not a substitute for firsthand experience in living and learning. Reading about democracy is not a valid alternative to the learning that comes from direct interaction with peers and the others in one's world.

How are new and socially useful meanings built? Experience shows us that children learn orderly living when they understand themselves in relation to their tasks and are able to work through them day after day. Living in a democratic society means living in a changing society. Adults help children achieve understanding of and skill in such living only by providing many opportunities for it. Deliberate planning and encouragement of positive learning at timely moments lets children take their own next steps. Literature may be an important part of the teacher's deliberate planning, and should be available for the children's choosing and accepting.

SUMMARY

Literature and social learning reinforce each other. The child turns to books for facts and for the language he needs to articulate his wants and needs. The emotional content of stories helps him relive his own feelings yet lets him escape from them. As he lives in the world of change, he finds security in the many kinds of literature available to him.

Making the teacher the model

in the literature experience

THE TEACHER AS A MODEL

The term *model* is selected for use as a key word here partly because, while it does possess a certain inspirational quality, it does not connote a demand for exactness of measurement, nor serve as a standard of perfection. A teacher dare not hope to be an *ideal*, nor do children really expect it of him. Such a role would keep him aloof and prevent him from taking part in the seething life of the classroom. Above all else, a teacher must be a warm, living reality for children, and the only avenue of communication open to him in this regard is his own natural and spontaneous behavior. The teacher as a model does not merely play a role; he does not perform mechanically from the script of a methods textbook; there are no prescribed directions to tell him when to smile, when to admonish, when to withdraw. These cues must come from within.

The art of becoming a teacher-model will not be mastered by even the best-calculated intellectual planning alone. If a teacher hopes to create in the classroom an emotional climate which encourages children to be themselves and to realize their own potentials, then he too must feel free to be himself. He should indeed feel that he is worthy of his children's emulation; an emulation of the spirit as well as of action. A teacher's real growth comes through his own experiences with children; of course he must be able to distinguish the true nature of these experiences, and then feel free to be guided by them.

This chapter is by JAMES E. HIGGINS, of the Levittown, New York, Public Schools.

Inherent within the teacher's naturalness is one of the basic strengths of good teaching—integrity. If, for instance, a teacher hopes to generate excitement concerning books and their content, he himself must feel strongly about them, for without such a foundation of honesty, all techniques are reduced to superficial gimmicks. This is not to rule out the value of trying out the suggestions of others who perhaps have had more experience; indeed there will be some specific suggestions for consideration in these pages, but it should be emphasized that the suggestions of others must always be tested and assimilated according to the teacher's own beliefs, temperament, and the teaching situation itself.

In the case of literature, it is the teacher's own feeling for books and their content which is the most significant factor in determining the success or failure of his program in a primary grade classroom. It is the chief task of the teacher of young children to spread the contagion of enjoyment to be found within books; for, say what you will, enjoyment is a basic commodity of literature, and it is also the foundation for later appreciation. It is the teacher's enthusiasm and general attitude towards books and reading which serve as the model for his children, not his particular preferences in the selection and presentation of material. To transmit this enthusiasm, of course, he must be quite at home with his material, and at the same time he must be willing to experiment; he must feel free to err in judgment from time to time. The atmosphere is healthiest when he is able to touch each of his pupils with a spark of excitement without encroaching upon the individuality of any one of them.

THE TEACHER SHOWS HE PRIZES BOOKS . . .

It is not enough that a teacher prize books and their content; it is his responsibility to communicate this feeling to his pupils.

How is it done?

Again *integrity,* or perhaps *sincerity,* is the clue.

Children are quick to know the teacher who prizes books . . .

. . . by the way he reads.

Reading aloud to the class is perhaps the medium most used by teachers in presenting a piece of literature to their children. Too often this activity is considered as time stolen from more important curricular considerations. It must be remembered that such reading is a form of drama, and, as such, it needs a dramatic presentation. The teacher who sees reading aloud as more than a quiet moment in the day's activity will be concerned about such things as the selection of material, interpretation of the story or poem, and problems of performance.

. . . by the way he handles the book itself.

Children should always be taught to respect property, be it their own or that of others, but the care and handling of a book goes much deeper than consideration of its material value. True, a book is an object of value whether it is read or not, but we are educating children to be readers rather than collectors of books. The magic quality of books relies upon the child's feeling of wonder concerning his own power as a reader of the printed word—when he discovers that it is his reading act which breathes life into the book, and makes of it something more than an object composed of paper and ink.

In our time we have surrounded children with reading material, to the extent that books have become rather commonplace in our everyday living. The primary grade teacher has the responsibility of helping to preserve this familiarity and warmness towards books, while at the same time, training children in the A B C's of book care. The success of this training will depend greatly upon how the teacher himself handles book material.

How does one communicate warmth and respect at the same time?— the same way that one finds it possible to transmit love and admiration through a handshake with an old friend.

. . . by the way he synchronizes literature with the everyday life of the classroom.

An appropriate story, poem, or anecdote, interjected at the fitting moment, is just the needed catalyst to change a common occurrence, such as the first spring rain or the return to class of Johnny who had the mumps, into a unique experience, tinged with wonder, delight, and excitement.

This kind of spontaneity can be achieved only through a close acquaintance with literary material, whether it be written especially for children or not. Indeed, much of the teacher's material will be garnered through experiences and channels not usually thought of as "educational."

. . . by the way he talks about books, and the way he seeks and accepts the children's reactions to their reading.

Everyone, child and adult alike, has his own special likes and dislikes in reading. Why then should a teacher be any exception? Children will feel better about discussing their own preferences, defending their own opinions, and acknowledging their own biases, if their teacher has already served as a model for this kind of openness and opinionatedness.

The teacher's animation during discussion, especially when he is talking about his favorite books, characters, descriptions, illustrations and the like, will also serve as a model for his children. A speaker who is aware of his audience, and who is concerned with their reactions, will also be a good listener. The teacher should always remember, however, that in the area of literature the interchange will be concerned mostly with feelings, opinions, ideas, and hunches, not with facts and certainties. For this kind of discussion, experience is indeed the best teacher; one learns best how to talk and how to listen to children by doing it.

. . . by the way he encourages independent reading.

If a teacher always equates teaching with instruction, then it is doubtful whether he will do much teaching of literature at the primary grade level. Most teachers are pressed by the many facets of the modern curriculum, so that *time* has become a very important consideration in planning the daily schedule. This sometimes results in the feeling on the part of some that the teacher must be always *doing,* or time is being wasted.

Independent, recreational reading is a "doing" activity, but it is the child who is engaged in the doing; what he needs most from his teacher is time and an atmosphere which will allow him to enter the world of his book. The question which the teacher must constantly answer for himself while he is planning his program is: Is literature a legitimate part of the school day, or is it not?

Children learn early that adults do more than talk about the things that are really important to them. No amount of pedagogical preaching will convince children of the joys to be found in recreational reading; they look to the teacher who will stimulate their sense of wonder and curiosity and then provide the time and opportunity for them to explore.

This same teacher will also help his children build a classroom library, as well as encourage them to make good use of all the facilities, such as school and public libraries, which make books and other literary materials available to them.

HOW THE TEACHER IMPROVES IN USING LITERATURE WITH CHILDREN

The teacher need not go far to find assistance to support his efforts in making books and their content exciting to children. There are:

Graduate and in-service courses in children's literature which will help him to develop new insights, seek new approaches, and become acquainted with new materials and media.

School librarians and children's librarians in local libraries, who are usually more than willing to give teachers and parents all the assistance they desire.

Professional literature (anthologies, critical reviews, bibliographies) and periodicals such as *Elementary English* and *The Horn Book,* to keep the teacher abreast of materials and practices in the world of children's literature.

Fellow teachers, who, through faculty meetings and more informal get-togethers, can be most helpful by sharing their experiences concerning books and children.

Children themselves can be the most help. By keeping a good ear open in the classroom, on the playground, and in the lunchroom, teachers can really discover the kinds of books and activities that the children are finding exciting.

The teacher's image of himself as a model in the literature experience for young children is of prime importance. It would be a great mistake for a teacher of young children not to realize how important professionally he is, for he serves as a model of an educated person in the young whom he teaches. He can make education in literature desirable in the eyes of his pupils, young as they may be.

Evaluating young children's experiences with literature

Are we able to evaluate children's literary experiences? Only in a partial way. We can observe children's reactions as they listen to a story or poem—we can see how absorbed they become in it, how their faces mirror the emotions they feel, how completely their attention is held. Through listening to them we can note whether they carry over the impressions received—what do they want to say about it? Later we listen to their comments about the classroom or playground—can we trace their ideas back to an experience with literature?

In the same way we can evaluate the literary experiences of the child who is reading for himself. How completely is he absorbed in the situation? Does his face mirror the emotions he is feeling? Does he seek out further reading that lets us know that past reading has been meaningful to him?

The following illustration of a classroom experience in literature is typical of a starting point in evaluating children's experiences with literature.

STORIES AND POEMS WITH CHILDREN

The chord struck on the piano notified the first graders that work time was over and things should be put away. Miss Ellis helped with a few tasks and then as she noted that many were ready, she picked up two books from her desk and moved to her chair in a quiet corner. The children who had finished gathered near her, making themselves comfortable on the floor.

This chapter is by CONSTANCE CARR McCUTCHEON, formely Editor of *Childhood Education.*

"What are you going to read to us today?" asked Joan. Miss Ellis held up the book, *Millions of Cats,* by Wanda Gág.

"What are those things on the cover?" asked Billy. Miss Ellis held the book closer to him, "Oh, cats! Sure are a lot of them."

"Yes, that is the name of the story, *Millions of Cats.*"

Joe began laughing boisterously. "Millions of cats? There couldn't be that many!"

Miss Ellis' voice was calm. "Remember, it is a story. But the name of it really makes us wonder." She looked about the room; all but three children had joined the group. "I believe we can begin. You people join us quietly as soon as you can."

With a warm, friendly voice she began to read. The group immediately quieted; however, two or three children were fidgeting. By the time the first two pages had been read and Miss Ellis stopped to show the pictures to the group, everyone was caught up into the story. As the story went on there were comments from the children about the pictures; Miss Ellis acknowledged the remarks with a smile or a nod of agreement but did not develop a discussion. She felt the story thread should not be interrupted during the reading.

As the last picture was seen, a contented sigh spread over the group. "Oh, that was a good story!" "Can we see the pictures again?" This time the comments on the pictures were picked up. And as the refrain from the story appeared, Miss Ellis said it and soon the children were chiming in with her to say,

> "Hundreds of cats,
> Thousands of cats,
> Millions and billions and trillions of cats." [1]

As interest in the discussion waned, Miss Ellis picked up the second book and said, "We have about ten more minutes for some poems. Which ones shall we say?"

"I have some new shoes," said Jilly shyly. And with glee the children began, "New shoes, new shoes."

After two or three other choices, Miss Ellis said, "I have some poems about snow. As she read "First Snow," by Mary Louise Allen, and "Winter," by Dorothy Aldis, there were appreciative chuckles at the word pictures. She ended up by reading "Velvet Shoes," by Elinor Wylie. The quiet in the room and the dreaminess on some of the faces were rewards in themselves. Quietly she dismissed the children in small groups to get their wraps.

[1] From *Millions of Cats,* by Wanda Gág. New York: Coward-McCann, 1928. Copyright 1928 by Coward-McCann, Inc.

How may Miss Ellis review the situation which has been presented? Let us begin by analyzing the situation for the story and poems. These first graders were accustomed to a storytime. Miss Ellis had established place and procedures for behavior which suited her purposes. She may see if they suit children's purposes by noting whether the children happily anticipate the "reading-together time." Are the children enthusiastic toward what will happen? Do they move quickly into customary situations for listening?

What observations can Miss Ellis make during the reading time? How did the children react to the story? Was there more or less of the usual absorption as the plot developed? Did their faces reflect the feelings invoked? Did their interpretation of pictures show an accurate impression of the mood and situation of the story? Did the story provoke ongoing discussion—that is, beyond the text of the story?

And what about the poetry? Did the children accept it as pleasurable experience? Did they participate happily in poems which they knew? Did they respond in mood to new poems presented?

As the story or poems conclude, do the children respond with the young child's benediction, "Tell it again!"

Throughout other parts of the school day do you hear references to the story, the repetition of some of the nonsense phrases or pithy wisdom? Do the children voluntarily act out plots? Do they incorporate ideas into their creative art experiences?

EVALUATION OF DEEPER VALUES

But the criteria thus far presented are only surface manifestations of what we hope literature will bring to each child. In order to evaluate the experiences with literature that the children have, we must decide what we feel literature can do for the child:

- Good literature catches the tune of the child's everyday life.

- It re-creates the world about him. It opens his eyes to see added dimensions. It stretches present meaning into new ideas—it interprets his experiences into meaningful concepts.

- Literature satisfies the child in his quest for knowledge, not only as interpretation of the present but as a means of living vicariously in the past or far away.

- Literature passes on to the child the cultural values of his society—the inherited truths of past generations.

- Literature can help the child to better understand himself, and to better understand other people.

- Literature stimulates the child's imagination, encourages the creative play of ideas.

- Good literature provides an outlet for the emotions—laughter, wonder, and a pulling of the heart strings.

- Through literature the wonder of words and their virtuosity in conveying ideas through rhythm and sound bring the satisfactions of any truly creative form of activity.

With these aims the teacher can evaluate. Yet no one encounter can achieve all the values of literature for the child. So we must investigate three areas: (1) We must know the child and his needs. (2) We must know good literature for children. (3) We must know a variety of ways of presenting literature.

Miss Ellis cannot hope to touch all the values of literature during one session of poems and stories. In the first place it takes a variety of literary materials to encompass all the values. In the second place this one experience has meant different things to different children in the group.

Each child brings a different background—in past literary experience and in his basic emotional needs. Even the situation of any particular day makes a difference in what an individual child may take from the experience. For instance, Johnny, who has a great need for being loved and accepted for himself, may be coming down with a cold and instead of taking in the concept of the kitten who became beautiful through love and care is only lulled by the rhythm of the words.

The child and his needs—the group and their needs. Children differ in their response to stories and poetry just as they differ in their tastes for food. Certainly the background of home experiences means that some children have been nourished on Mother Goose and all the old folk tales. There are other children who have hardly heard a Mother Goose rhyme and to whom all the familiar stories are new. The teacher who recognizes a great spread of literary experience among the children will want to present stories and poems that encompass all the needs—some of the old familiar tales now and then (children love to hear old favorites again) and some new, lead-on stories and poems. For children who are able to read, the provision of good books for all needs and free reading time solves many problems.

Some children respond more enthusiastically to one type of story than another. Some children are carried away with "make believe," while other children feel such stories are just a little queer. So the teacher will need to have a balance between types of literary material.

Children know what they like in literature, but they do not know everything they *might* like. The alert teacher provides stimulating literature in many categories. One second grade teacher who had a very advanced group who were voraciously reading simple biographies chose some highly fanciful stories for "story time."

But just as children differ, so do groups of children differ. The teacher must vary story presentations from one year to the next.

Good literature. In order to evaluate children's literary experience the teacher must recognize good children's literature and the usual development of literary taste in children. Recognizing good children's literature is a time-saver for the teacher, it weeds out material of little value and uses the time for sharing really good books and poems. Every teacher needs his own criteria for judging the worth of material to be presented. For instance, this writer feels that it is a waste of time for a teacher to read a "Bobbsey Twin book" to the group. Yet she recognizes that some children may reach a stage when they can hardly wait to finish one Bobbsey Twin book in order to begin another. The time of the whole group might better be spent on Lois Lenski's regional stories.

The teacher needs to know the usual development of literary taste in children. The Mother Goose rhymes have been beginning poetry for many children for many years because of the rhythms, the rhymes, and the play involved in them. Very young children respond to rhythm and sound of nonsense words and are not disturbed by lack of logical meaning. Early experiences with books are usually in identifying pictures—a language growing experience. The simple "here and now" stories are usual beginning stories, as are the fanciful stories with easy identification such as Peter Rabbit. Children may enjoy the Dr. Seuss nonsense yet not be ready for the more sophisticated nonsense of William Pène du Bois.

If a teacher recognizes that children move from simple plots to more complex, if he recognizes that attention spans increase so that longer stories can be included, then the evaluation of children's responses can be more objective. A first grade teacher was let down when her six-year-olds did not respond with enthusiasm and interest to "Sleeping Beauty." The fault lay not in the story but rather in the background of the children, who had not had kindergarten experience.

Variety in presentation. The teacher needs to recognize and use a variety of means of presenting literature to children. Too often the teacher relies entirely on reading to children. Some children will experience stories and poems more deeply by seeing them come alive in play, or in partaking in an acting-out experience. Storytelling is one of the closest three-way relationships that can exist between teacher, child, and story. Choral speaking, audio-visual aids, records, and even television programs all give added dimensions to children's experiences.

HOW DO WE KNOW?

We can evaluate young children's experience with literature only partially. These are some of the guides for consideration:

- We must know the child and his needs and how those needs can be met by literature.

- We can provide the child with a wealth of literature old and new and encompassing the many categories into which literature falls.

- We can provide time and situations for literature—group time and individual time.

- We can provide literature through a variety of ways.

- We can assess the child's reponse and enthusiasm—how completely he gives his attention.

- We can note the child's developing values that he gives to different literary material—his growing literary taste.

- We can note the child's willingness to investigate literature that is new to him in form or format.

- We can be most satisfied to find the child turning to literature to meet further needs.

No, we can only partially evaluate what happens within the child. At best, we can give him the very best literature we know. We must continue to grow in our own appreciation of literature for children by watching and learning from them. Then, planting our seeds in the depths of their lives, we may harvest an occasional blossom without knowing the strength of the roots.